Books of the Theatre Series

Number 2   *August 1960*

A Rare Books of the Theatre project of the
American Educational Theatre Association

ADOLPHE APPIA'S

"The Work of Living Art"

A THEORY OF THE THEATRE

Translated by H. D. Albright

and

"MAN IS THE MEASURE OF ALL THINGS"

Translated by Barnard Hewitt

Edited by Barnard Hewitt

UNIVERSITY OF MIAMI PRESS

Coral Gables, Florida

Copyright © 1960 by
Walther R. Volbach
Library of Congress Catalog Card Number 60-13830
ISBN 0-87024-007-2
Second printing, 1966
Third printing, 1969
Fourth printing, 1975

Manufactured in the United States of America

CONTENTS

---

[1] Published in *La Revue Théâtrale*, VIII (1954), No. 25, pp. 7-15.

FOREWORD

As THE SECOND VOLUME in the American Educational Theatre Association—University of Miami Press Books of the Theatre Series, we are pleased to present in English for the first time Adolphe Appia's *The Work of Living Art*, for, although it is not so well known as his *La Mise en Scène du Drame Wagnèrien* or his *La Musique et la Mise en Scène* (published in German translation as *Die Musik und die Inscenierung*), it was written nearly twenty years later and is a much more complete statement of Appia's mature theory of theatre art. He called it his most significant work, the work which expressed his ideas most completely.[1]

The brief essay "Man is the Measure of All Things" expounds essentially the same aesthetic without the detailed support which Appia presents in *The Work of Living Art*.

We are indebted to the *Fondation Adolphe Appia*, Geneva, Switzerland, for permission to publish these two works. We are grateful also to Edmund Stadler and the *Schweizerische Theatersammlung*, Berne, Switzerland, for the portrait photograph of Adolphe Appia by Thérèse Appia which precedes the section of designs in this volume.

The editor and the translators are grateful to Walther R. Volbach of Texas Christian University, who, acting for both the *Fondation Adolphe Appia* and the American Educational Theatre Association, read the translations and made many helpful suggestions. Mr. Volbach, who is translating Appia's essays, also contributed the note on page 107.

The late A. M. Drummond of Cornell University assisted greatly in the early stages of the translation of *The Work of*

---

[1]"Curriculum Vitae d'Adolphe Appia," written by himself in 1927, unpublished manuscript in the possession of the *Fondation Adolphe Appia*.

Living Art. During the recent revision, F. B. Agard, Division of Modern Languages, Cornell University, gave valuable advice on the rendering of a number of passages. W. H. Rothrock and Michael Winesanker of Texas Christian University and Lee Simonson made helpful suggestions regarding both translations. Claude P. Viens of the Department of French, University of Illinois, assisted in the same way on "Man is the Measure of All Things."

BARNARD HEWITT

ADOLPHE APPIA AND
"THE WORK OF LIVING ART"

H. D. ALBRIGHT

OF APPIA'S PUBLISHED VOLUMES, *The Work of Living Art* best represents his mature view of the art of the theatre. Here we see, and perhaps come to understand, Appia the aesthetician—as opposed, let us say, to Appia the reformer of the *mise en scène*. It is of course in this latter role that he has been widely known in the past, at least partially because interested students have usually had so fragmentary an acquaintance with the main body of his writing. Actually, Appia's various proposals for reforming scenic and lighting conventions — through which his influence has largely been felt — were, in his own view, secondary to a larger purpose: the formulation of a new aesthetic of the theatre, the basis for a new art form. At a relatively early stage in his thinking, when he was still strongly influenced by Wagner, Appia conceived of this new form as "word-tone drama"; later on, particularly in the volume with which we are now concerned, he saw it as "living art." The career of this unusual man and sensitive artist spanned some of the most interesting and exciting decades in theatrical history. The development of his artistic life, and of the conceptions which gave it purpose and direction, paralleled the development of the new theatre and stagecraft which we now take for granted. Both his life and the central aspects of his work deserve to be better known.

Adolphe Appia was born at Geneva, Switzerland, on September 1, 1862. His father, Louis-Paul Appia, though born in Hanau (in Prussia), was a naturalized Swiss, and spent more than half his life at Geneva. Holding degrees in medicine from both Heidelberg and Paris, the elder Appia was well known as a surgeon; the author of several books in his special field, wartime surgery, he was one of the founders of the original Red Cross Society. Adolphe Appia had one sister, Hélène; and one brother, Paul, a banker in Geneva. A cousin, Paul-Henri, was a theologian, and a nephew, Theodore, was a musician and teacher in New York City.[1] Another nephew, Edmond, a musician and conductor in Geneva, is director of the *Fondation Adolphe Appia,* which is preserving Appia's papers and which still controls the rights to his published work.

Reared in Geneva, Adolphe Appia attended school there, apparently only mildly interested in a "formal" education. Even as a youth, he was reported to be deeply religious—in the broadest sense—and to betray the nature of a mystic and a dreamer. Before the age of fifteen, he read books on art, music, and the theatre. He was especially interested in, and deeply influenced by, the music of Bach and Beethoven; the latter's "Ninth Symphony," it is said, constituted his "initiation into art." After completing his secondary schooling, he studied music at Leipzig, Dresden, and Vienna. He spent considerable time at Bayreuth, where his growing interest in opera in general and in Wagnerian music-drama in particular was most fully developed. From the time he had seen his first opera (Gounod's *Faust*), he had been discontented and indeed disillusioned with the staging of musical drama. His visits to Bayreuth aggravated the discontent and sharpened his desire to devote himself further to that area of interest.

Consequently, his first book,[2] published in 1895, was on the subject of Wagnerian staging. Wagner, Appia believed, was content to rely on the contemporary conventions in staging and design, with their realistically painted drops and flats, even

---

[1] I am indebted to Theodore Appia for some of the biographical material used here. I have relied heavily also on a *curriculum vitae,* written by Appia himself in 1927, and furnished by the *Fondation Adolphe Appia,* Geneva. Other biographical sources were: *The Historical and Biographical Dictionary of Switzerland* (Neuchatel, 1921) and *The Italian Encyclopedia of Science, Arts, and Letters* (Rome, 1929).
[2] *La Mise en Scène du Drame Wagnérian* (Paris: Chailley, 1895).

though these were foreign to the expressive nature of the music-dramas themselves. Appia almost wholly renounced painting in stage settings, and advocated a system of essentially three-dimensional units and a pattern of controlled and plastic light which he claimed were organically related to the Wagnerian drama and its action.

In elemental form, this early work set forth many of the aesthetic principles which were later to make Adolphe Appia famous. These principles were further enlarged and developed in what is in some ways his best-known work, *Music and Theatrical Production*—which, though published in German in 1899, had been written in French a few years earlier.[1] In this volume are presented or suggested almost all of the production theories now familiarly associated with Appia's name, most of which were essentially original with him, and many of which are by this time generally applied, both here and abroad. Chief among the principles of production laid down in *Music and Theatrical Production* are these: the aesthetic validity of plastic and three-dimensional settings, as opposed to those painted in two dimensions; the need for organic unity between play, setting, and action; the primary and fundamental importance of the actor and his movement in space; the possibilities of music as an expressive element and as a factor of control; and—perhaps most influential of all—the expressive and unifying power of light.

From varying points of view, several efforts have been made within the past three decades to outline and summarize, in English, portions of Appia's aesthetic beliefs;[2] and, almost without exception, these have been based primarily on *Music and Theatrical Production* rather than on the author's later work. All have agreed on the validity, the significance, and the influence of those beliefs. Lee Simonson, writing in 1932, insisted that "the first hundred and twenty pages [of *Music and Theatrical*

---

[1]*La Musique et la Mise en Scène;* published as *Die Musik und Die Inscenierung* (Munich: Bruckmann, 1899).
[2]E.g., Chapter IV, Part III, of Lee Simonson, *The Stage Is Set* (New York, 1932); in an Appia memorial issue of *Theatre Arts* (Vol. 16, 1932); and in W. R. Fuerst and S. J. Hume, *Twentieth Century Stage Decoration* (London, 1928).

Production] are nothing less than the textbook of modern stage-craft";[1] and, again, that "most of what we call innovation or experiment is a variation of Appia's ideas, deduced from his original premises."[2]

It should be stressed, however, that—at least according to Appia's intention—these general principles of staging and design were secondary to a central purpose that is commonly overlooked or ignored. Appia's primary motive was to discover a means or a method that would insure the full realization, in the theatre, of Wagnerian music-drama and of a new form (partially based on Wagner) which he himself hoped to develop. For this latter art form, "word-tone drama," Appia set up in *Music and Theatrical Production* what he called a hierarchy of expression, in which music was the controlling factor.

Appia believed that the word-tone drama should tend toward the presentational rather than the representational, and (like music itself, as he saw it) toward the "expressive" rather than the intellectually meaningful. The means-of-expression in the new form were to be, first, the actor (through voice and movement); and second, the stage setting (through light, color, line, and mass). There were to be two requirements for these means-of-expression: they were to be definitely under the control of the dramatist; and their elements were to be organically related. In Appia's view, the music of the word-tone drama could control the actor, inasmuch as it could control his voice and his movements. Moreover, since the living body of the actor determined the nature of the setting, the music could—through the actor—control the setting. Finally, living and ambient light, like music a direct expression of the soul of the drama, could unite actor and setting, in a single, organic whole.

In such an art form, conceived according to such a hierarchy of expression, most of the principles of production for which Appia is popularly known are essentially by-products, secondary to a larger central purpose. Properly viewed, that is

[1] Simonson, *The Stage Is Set*, pp. 354-355.
[2] Ibid., p 377.

to say, *Music and Theatrical Production* is an exploratory essay on the road to Appia's formulation of a new aesthetic of the theatre—never fully developed or realized, so far as Appia was concerned, and never fully understood or accepted by those who undertook to follow his work.

In any case, Appia devoted most of his attention, from 1900 on, to theatrical designing and staging. It is fortunate that many of his designs are available, both in his published works and in various reference books on stage decoration; especially valuable is a set of fifty-five of Appia's designs, published after his death.[1] His first practical experience in staging was apparently gained in 1903, when the Comtesse de Bearn put at his disposal a large hall in her home in Paris. Here, for a short time, he was guaranteed reasonable financial freedom and a small but interested audience. Among the presentations at this theatre in Paris were scenes from Byron's *Manfred* (music by Schumann) and from the opera *Carmen*.

As early as 1899, in *Music and Theatrical Production*, Appia had foreseen a kind of "musical gymnastics" which he hoped would ultimately be included in the professional training of actors. In 1906 he found—in Emile Jaques-Dalcroze's experiments at Geneva—promise of the fulfillment of such a hope. The Dalcroze system, which is now known as Eurythmics, has as a guiding principle the relationship between the rhythm of a man's physical body and what might be called the rhythm of his inner being.[2] Appia's next ten years were spent largely in collaboration with Dalcroze; while the latter was developing his theory of Eurythmics, Appia was developing the theory of dramatic art and dramatic production which he was ultimately to outline in *The Work of Living Art,* here published in English for the first time. In addition to designing settings for many Dalcroze recitals and demonstrations (both at Geneva and at Hellerau), Appia staged several major productions in collaboration with Dalcroze:

---

1 *Adolphe Appia* (A Portfolio), Intro., Henry C. Bonifas (Zürich: Orell-Fussli, 1929).
2 Disciples of Dalcroze believe that a careful and continued application of Eurythmic theories will not only result in aesthetic and hygienic bodily development, but will exert a positive influence on the character and philosophy of the student.

Glück's *Orpheus and Eurydice* and Claudel's *The Tidings Brought to Mary* at Hellerau in 1913, and the June Festival, a patriotic pageant and spectacle, at Geneva in 1914. The settings as well as the general mode of staging in these productions conformed closely to his maturing views.

Many extant designs illustrate Appia's conception of theatre art during this period of collaboration with Dalcroze. The rationale behind this conception is best revealed, however, in the last of his major publications, *The Work of Living Art*, which appeared in Geneva in 1921. In this volume, he reorganized his aesthetic theories, explaining their origin and predicting their future. Like its more familiar predecessor, the book is largely devoted to the basis for a new art form—in this case what Appia calls "living art," which is in some respects a development of the "word-tone drama" described in his *Music and Theatrical Production;* but the basic concepts of the theatre art which were suggested or outlined in that earlier work are here sharpened and clarified. A year before his death, Appia wrote that he considered *The Work of Living Art* to be the most significant of his publications and that in his view it most completely expressed his mature thought.

Briefly summarized, the later volume insists on the living body of the actor as a point-of-departure. Reiterating Appia's earlier conception of music as an expressive and controlling force, it sets forth his proposals for the "living" art, whose social influence, he believed, should and would become universal. Finally, it indicates a tendency toward increased simplification in stage settings, reasserts the expressive and unifying power of light, and urges the closest of rapport between audience and actor. Since the body of the actor and its rhythmic movements are—in Appia's final view—the primary factor in theatre art, the chief if not the only purpose of stage decoration is to express weight and solidity and thus to offer a contrast to the living body and its movements. The ideal stage setting is a "rhythmic space," and little more.

This treatise was followed in 1923 by a shorter one, *Liv-*

ing Art or Dead Nature?[1] which enlarged on Appia's ideas regarding the "living" art and paid further attention to what he believed to be its social implications. In the same year Appia was invited to Milan to stage *Tristan and Isolde* at La Scala. His settings for this Wagnerian work, largely because of their extreme simplicity and their almost classic lines, were not well received by the public.[2] Appia's last staging projects were done at Basle in 1924-25, for *The Rhinegold* and *The Valkyrie*, from Wagner's *Ring*, and the *Prometheus* of Aeschylus./His designs, which were in large part the basis of his early reputation, were included in exhibitions over a period of almost twenty years: Darmstadt (1909); Zürich (International Exposition, 1914); Cologne (1914); Geneva (1918); Amsterdam (International Exposition, 1922); London (International Exposition, 1922); Milan (1923); Stockholm (1924); Basle (1924); Zürich (1925); Leipzig (1925); and Magdeburg (1927).

Although he may have planned to publish still another book, he never brought that task to completion. The student or the scholar must judge his work from the designs, a number of which are reproduced here; from his three published volumes, of which the present one best represents the convictions of his lifetime; from the brief accounts of his practical work in the theatre itself; and from his scattered articles, many of which were never published, and most of which are in any case unavailable in English.

Appia's influence—on theatre aesthetics as well as on stage lighting and design—is by this time unquestioned, both here and in Europe. As all but the most casual observer is aware, he is usually named with Gordon Craig (and occasionally with Georg Fuchs and others) as one of the prophets of the New

---

[1] *Art Vivant ou Nature Morte?* (Milan: Bottega di Poesia, 1923). This essay was first published in *Wendigen*, 9 and 10 (Double Number, 192i), an issue devoted to the International Exposition of Theatre Arts held in Amsterdam early in 1922. It has since been translated by S. A. Rhodes in *Theatre Annual*, II (1943), pp. 38-45.
[2] It is interesting to note that Gordon Craig defends Appia's work at La Scala, contending that he was given neither the support nor the freedom necessary for realization of his ideas. On this point, see: Craig, *Fourteen Notes* (U. of Washington Quarto, No. II), Seattle, 1931, pp. 10-11.

Stagecraft of the present century. Writing as late as 1949, I expressed my own conviction that

> as to theory, he clarified the aesthetic of musical drama in general, and shed new light on Wagnerian criticism in particular. As to practice, he prophesied the intensified expressiveness and the unity of effect typical of the best of twentieth-century production, and foresaw the three-dimensional stage and the plastic, ambient light that have become accepted norms for the twentieth-century scene . . . Adolphe Appia set the staging pattern—or was first articulate about the staging pattern—which still remains with us. The expressive or evocative or suggestive realism which he in a sense introduced into the conventional theatres of our time has not yet run its course. His new and truly unified dramatic form, his new and presentational theatre building, his new and communal art of the future we have largely passed over or have found "impractical." But the relatively simplified and expressive and essentially anti-natural stagecraft and lighting, of which he was an early advocate and indeed practitioner, we have continued to develop (some would say exploit) through our present decade.[1]

Never content to live far from Geneva for any length of time, Appia spent the last years of his life near that city, in an old castle on the Lake. From the castle's windows he could look down on the terraced vineyards of Vevey; within and near its walls he was free from the crowds that oppressed him. Here, unmarried, he quietly entertained those who sought him out.[2] It was his nature to believe firmly in all his fellow men, and to seek—in things and in men—the "inner being of all outward seeming." Extremely retiring, he shunned every form of publicity. He knew few people intimately; he was known intimately by

---

[1] H. Darkes Albright, "Appia Fifty Years After," *Quarterly Journal of Speech*, Vol. 35 (1949), pp. 303 and 188.

[2] In these last days he was robust and heavily bearded, with kindly but piercing eyes shining out beneath heavy brows, as the portrait in this volume shows.

even fewer. A great artist and a generous and kindly man, he possessed both the virtues and faults of an intense idealist. All who came in contact with him testify to his greatness of spirit.

Appia died on February 29, 1928; and, in accordance with his wishes, he was buried near Geneva.

ADOLPHE APPIA'S

"The Work of Living Art"

Translated by H. D. Albright

TO

Emile Jaques-Dalcroze
the faithful friend to whom I owe my aesthetic homeland

. . . and to you
        oh, Walt Whitman
        who will understand me, since you are *living* — always!

ADOLPHE APPIA

"Camerado! this is no book;
Who touches this, touches a man . . ."
        WALT WHITMAN

PREFACE

THIS STUDY was originally twice its present length. The author once believed that he could clarify and simplify his concepts if he documented them at every step and developed them fully. He had hoped by this means to express the essence of his thought, but in the course of his investigation he soon found that essence inexpressible—at least in this fashion. Moreover, he was gradually compelled to realize that one cannot entice a companion, however amiable and indulgent, to pursue an unfamiliar path for reasons unknown to him in advance, if — by continually reminding him of the main traveled road and its familiar aspects —one turns his glances, and perhaps his steps as well, away from the new and unknown route.

In every sphere of life documentation is a study that is accomplished while standing still. It is a preparation for the voluntary act of departure. The legs of Rodin's "Man Walking" were "documented"; that is why they were ready to begin walking. A tourist stops to consult his map; then he folds it up, and starts out along the route which he feels he now understands.

The author has spent many years consulting others and questioning himself. Irresistibly drawn toward an unknown which he sensed to be marvelous, he wished nonetheless to safeguard himself in every way before committing himself to the quest. He realized that when he did commit himself it would be final; his first vague presentiment of that gradually became a conviction: *to turn back would be impossible,* and yet he had to begin the journey.

Accordingly he did begin it. Behind him were broken, one by one, the precious links binding him to a past which he had thought he would never need to, still less be able to, abandon.

The aim of this work is to offer the reader a preparation, as it were, for a similar journey, and in this way to enable him to share in the author's "documentation" without sharing the author's hesitations or anxieties. To change one's course and thereby give up the known, which he loves, for an unknown which he cannot yet love, is to perform an act of faith. In any sphere of life a conversion—which means, rightly speaking, a change of course—is necessarily a serious and always a sorrowful event, since it involves discarding many possessions, a kind of progressive self-divestment, without any apparent replacements or compensations. This is all the more true inasmuch as ordinarily one is unwilling to discard anything at all, unless he has previously been convinced of the insufficiency or the unworthiness of what he is renouncing.

To return to what we have called our documentation, it is obvious that the author of a well-planned guide will facilitate your voyage not by offering a vague and general description of the region you are to pass through, but by giving you exact information—technical information. It is for you to decide, then, whether you have done well to undertake the journey.

In this expedition the author is at the same time both guide and traveler, and this study has a correspondingly twofold character: as a technical treatise, it assumes responsibility; as an itinerary, it invites confidence. But since it mainly discusses a question of aesthetics, the technical side will always dominate. That is inevitable, since art cannot be definitely analyzed and described; and for that reason this study will be extremely difficult.

The author asks the reader to pardon him in advance, and to bear in mind that the greatest and deepest joy that art can afford us is tragic in its essence; for, while art has the power to make us "live" our life without at the same time undergoing its sufferings, yet art demands in return—if we are to enjoy it profoundly—that we have suffered.

Adolphe Appia

Chexbres, May 1919

1. THE ELEMENTS

THE VERY LANGUAGE we use can often help us to clarify our own mental attitudes, and can provide us with the key to certain problems. Ordinarily, we express ourselves loosely, paying little attention to our language patterns as such. As a result, our thinking lacks the precision which full linguistic awareness could help to supply. Here is an example relevant to the present study.

Under the term "Art" we group various manifestations of our life; but if we are required to distinguish sharply between them, we let language come to our aid. Thus, we have the fine arts: painting, sculpture, and architecture; but we rarely say "the art of painting," "the art of sculpture," or "the art of architecture," unless we are being purposely analytical. For everyday usage, the name of the art itself is enough. We speak also of "poetry," though we usually fail to place it among the fine arts—a judgment that is only proper, since the beauty of words and of their arrangement acts only indirectly on our senses. Then, too, we use the term "poetics," which more specifically implies the technique of poetry, without requiring us to place either this technique or its aesthetic results under the heading of fine arts. These distinctions are clear; we need only be conscious of them whenever we use the terms.

But there is one art form which cannot be classed either among the fine arts or under poetry (or literature)—but which, nonetheless, should rank as an art in every sense of the word. I refer, of course, to *dramatic art*. Here, again, language attempts to orient us. The word "dramaturgy," which we use rarely and with a bit of distaste, is to dramatic art what poetics is to poetry.

It is concerned exclusively with the technique of the dramatist, indeed with only a part of that technique.

Here, then, is an important art form which we can satisfactorily name only by including the word "art." Why?

To begin with, we must note the extraordinary complexity of this art form, a complexity which is a result of the large number of mediums it must blend together in a homogeneous whole. Dramatic art requires first of all a text (with or without music); that is its relation to literature (or to music). This text is entrusted to human beings, who recite it or sing it as they bring it to life on the stage; that is its relation to sculpture and to painting, if we except the painting of scenery, which we shall discuss later on. Finally, architecture can also, to a certain degree, be related to the actor, as well as to the spectator; for the auditorium assumes a place in dramatic art on the basis of the latter's optical and acoustical requirements. Here, however, architecture is absolutely subordinated to specific ends which concern it only indirectly. Dramatic art seems, therefore, to borrow certain elements from each of the other arts. Is it possible to assimilate them?

Thanks to this complexity, our conception of dramatic art is always a bit confused. We are held up at the outset by the need for composing a text—a text expressing human emotions in a way that we can comprehend. But after our momentary hesitation on this point—certainly an essential one—we feel, with some embarrassment, that there is beyond this text, whatever it may be, something that is an integral part of dramatic art. It is an element we do not yet fully and exactly understand, and one we are inclined to count unimportant, possibly because we have such difficulty in focusing our attention on it. Quite casually, we call it the *mise en scène,* and then hurriedly close the parentheses which we had only just opened to insert this subtle and troublesome idea. Just as we do with other irksome work, we turn over the *mise en scène* to specialists, vaguely feeling that after all it is their affair; and then, with renewed peace of mind, turn back to the script of dramatic art. This, at least, does not distress us, and for that reason it seems within the compass of our critical analysis.

But working this way, are we not—almost in spite of ourselves—the least bit uneasy? Are we never going to face squarely the entire concept of dramatic art? And if we ever have the courage to do just that—like M. Emile Faguet, in his fine book, *Le Drame Ancien, Le Drame Moderne*—are we not fully aware of the exact moment when we are going to run out of breath? Again like M. Faguet, are we not going to drop a part of our burden as soon as it seems decently possible, and devote our analysis to what we can more easily carry?

The aim of this work is precisely to analyze those factors in dramatic art over which we tend to slip too discreetly; and to clarify and sharpen our ideas on those factors, by examining whatever matters of an aesthetic nature seem essential to the progress and evolution of the art.

A dangerous aphorism has misled us, and still misleads us. Trustworthy authorities have asserted that dramatic art is the harmonious combination of all the arts, and that such a combination must ultimately create a unified work of art—if, indeed, it has not done so already. They have even provisionally named this product "the art form of the future."

Such an idea is tempting—tempting because of the soothing simplification it so readily offers; and we have eagerly accepted this nonsense. Nothing in the artistic life of our times justifies it; our concerts, our art exhibitions, our architecture, our literature, even our theatres deny it. We sense that it is false; we are almost positive that it is false. Yet we persist in laying our critical sense to rest on this pillow of idleness, released from any further comprehension of the nature of artistic expression. For it is obvious that if we warp a definition to this degree by making it include things that have nothing whatever to do with it, then at the same time we are going to warp our own judgment of these things considered separately.

If dramatic art is to be merely a harmonious combination or union of all the other arts, then I no longer understand anything at all about any of them, and still less about dramatic art. Chaos is complete.

What, then, so totally differentiates each of our arts, even literature, from the mutually subordinated elements that make up dramatic art? Let us examine the arts in relation to that question.

In certain circumstances, favorable as to color, light, or form, a stage picture can suggest a *painting* or a *sculptured* group. In like circumstances so far as declamation (or song or orchestration) is concerned, we can approximate for a moment —for only a moment—pleasure that is purely *literary* (or purely *musical*). Seated comfortably and in a completely passive state of mind, we scarcely notice the *architecture* of the auditorium. It escapes our conscious attention, at least; and the transient fictions of the stage settings suggest only very indirectly the art of mass and of weight. In a confused way, we realize the presence of an unknown element that escapes our conscious thought at the very moment it is affecting our emotions and is dominating our receptive faculties. We hear and see, we listen and contemplate, putting off until later any pursuit of the mystery. Then, afterwards, the effort to re-visualize the production in its entirety fatigues us. We give up searching our memories (now too fragmentary and too concerned with the intellectual content of the piece) for the elusive something that has disturbed us all evening; and each new experience finds us similarly distracted, until we completely abandon the search.

Meanwhile museums and exhibitions are open; architecture, literature, and music are easily accessible. We fly from one to the other, desperately hoping that we can pilfer the secret from among their treasures; but all this time we are without peace of mind, and let us admit it frankly, without real pleasure.

Dramatic art, like the other arts, is directed to our eyes, our ears, our understanding—in short, to our whole being. Why are all our efforts at synthesis frustrated, almost before we start?

Can our artists shed any light on the problem?

Pen in hand, the poet *fixes* his dream on paper. On paper he fixes the poem's rhythms, its sounds, and its dimensions. The poem is to be read or declaimed; and it, in turn, is "fixed" in the eyes of the reader, on the lips of the declaimer. Brush in hand, the painter *fixes* his vision, just as he wishes to interpret it. The canvas or the wall determines its dimensions; color immobilizes its lines and movements, its lights and shades. In his imagination, the sculptor *halts* forms and their movements at the exact moment he desires; then he immobilizes them in clay, in stone, or in bronze. Through his designs, the architect *fixes* the dimensions, the arrangements, and the form of what he is planning to construct. On the pages of his score, the musician *fixes* sounds and their rhythm; he can even limit—with mathematical precision— their intensity and, above all, their duration. A poet can of course only approximate such a result, since the reader can at his own pleasure read rapidly or slowly.

We have this much, then, from the artists whose combined activity ought to constitute the height of dramatic art: a poetical text, definitely fixed; and examples of painting, sculpture, architecture, and music, each of these in turn definitely fixed. Put all of them on the stage, and we will have: poetry and music, which are developed in time; and painting, sculpture, and architecture, which are realized—and immobilized—in space. How can we possibly reconcile the individual life of each of these arts with a unified and harmonious whole!

Is there, perhaps, a way to achieve such harmonious agreement? Do time and space possess some reconciling element, some common denominator? Can form in space be manifested in successive time-durations, and can these time-durations, in turn, be expressed in terms of space? For if we wish to unite the arts of time and the arts of space in one single object, then our problem is reduced to this form.

In space, units of time are expressed by a succession of forms, hence by movement. In time, space is expressed by a succession of words and sounds, that is to say by varying time-durations prescribing the extent of the movement.

Movement—mobility—is the determining and conciliating principle which can so regulate the union of the several art forms that they will converge, as it were, at a given point and a given time, in dramatic art. Unique and imperative, this principle can organize these art forms hierarchically, can mutually and proportionately subordinate them, and can finally achieve a harmony that in themselves they would have sought in vain.

Here we are at the heart of the matter: how are we to apply the principle of movement to the fine arts, which are inherently immobile? How are we to apply it to poetry and especially to music, which are equally immobile in regard to space? Each of these arts owes its perfection, its unique completeness, to its very immobility. If we take that away from them, will we not destroy their *raison d'être,* or at least their inherent value?

A second question arises at this point: its solution will shape the course of both our inquiry and our reasoning. Movement is not an element in itself; it is a state or mode of being. What we must determine, then, is which elements in our art forms can possibly surrender the immobility which is so inherently a part of their nature.

Perhaps we shall gain some useful ideas in regard to this question if, ignoring for the moment the form of the individual arts—arts we are certain must be organically united to create the supreme work of art—we consider that fusion as already realized on a stage. Let us admit this hypothesis, and this leads us to define, first of all, what a stage is.

A stage is an empty and more or less illuminated space of arbitrary dimensions. A portion of one of the walls bounding the stage space opens on an auditorium set aside for spectators, and this opening forms a rigid frame beyond which seats are arranged in a definite order. Only the stage space is capable of redisposition and consequently should be equipped for frequent change. It can be lighted in one way or another; and the objects to be placed on it will need light to make them visible. The stage space, then, is in a state of latent power as regards both space and light.

Thus the stage embraces, potentially and by definition, two of the primary elements in our synthesis, space and light.

Let us now consider movement on the stage. It is as useful to the text and to music—that is, to the arts of time—as it is to immobile objects in space; it is the only possible unifying agent. Through movement the synthesis we have so far merely talked of can become a reality. But how?

The living and mobile body of the actor represents movement in space; it therefore plays a critical role. Without a text (which may be with or without music), dramatic art cannot exist; and the actor is the bearer of this text. Without movement, the other arts cannot take part in the dramatic action. In one hand, so to speak, the actor bears the text; in the other, as in a sheaf, he holds the arts of space. Irresistibly he brings his two hands together, and by movement creates the complete work of art. The living body is thus the real creator of the supreme art, holding as it does the secret of the hierarchical relations between the conflicting elements, because it stands at their head. When we seek, therefore, the place of the other arts in dramatic art, we must maintain the living and plastic body as our point of departure.

The body is not only mobile: it is plastic as well. This plasticity naturally gives it an immediate kinship with architecture and brings it close to sculptural form—without, however, fully identifying itself with sculpture, which is immobile. On the other hand, it is alien to the nature of painting. A plastic object demands lights and shadows that are real and positive. Placed before a painted ray of light or a painted shadow-projection, the plastic body stubbornly remains in its own atmosphere, its own light and shadow. The same is true of forms expressed in painting. These forms are not plastic, but two-dimensional, and the body is three-dimensional; their juxtaposition is out of the question.

The human body makes painted forms and painted light irrelevant on the stage.

What remains, then, of painting, since after all it must apparently play some part in the supreme art? Color, probably. But color does not belong exclusively to painting; indeed, the theory may be advanced that in painting color is only fictitious, since it is called upon to immobilize an instant of light, but is utterly unable to follow a ray or a shadow in its course. Living color, however, is so closely allied with light that it is difficult to separate them, and since light is in the highest degree mobile, living color will be equally so. Here we are far indeed from painting. For, if color in painting is fictitious, light is equally so; and since all that painting can expect from light is visibility, it has no concern at all with living light. A well-lighted painting is an unreal ensemble of forms, colors, lights, and shadows, prominently and clearly presented on a flat surface and placed in a favorable position. But that is all.

The absence of plasticity robs painting of one of the most powerful and marvelously expressive elements of our sensory life: light. And yet we would organically unite painting with the living body! We would grant it a rank in the stage hierarchy, as though its quality as a fine art obliged us to include it in the complete art—continually deceived, as we are, by the idea that the complete art consists merely of a union of all the other arts.

Now we have our finger, so to speak, on the gross falsity of that theory. Either painting must renounce its fictitious character in favor of the living body, a condition which is equivalent to suppressing its very nature; or the body must renounce its plastic and mobile life and must grant to painting a rank superior to its own, a condition which is the negation of dramatic art. As a result, we have no choice.*

But is it really necessary to renounce completely every-

*It is perhaps unnecessary to remark that current practice has chosen in favor of painting.

thing that painting has to offer? Let us recall that its limitations are its guarantee of perfection; and that this static perfection allows us to contemplate at leisure a transient state of nature or daily life, and to observe a multitude of relationships and gradations. Moreover, this instant has been carefully selected from among all the rest; it is a *chosen specimen*—which fact implies on the part of painting a kind of interpretation to which the mobile plasticity of the living body can never aspire. But let us go even further. The painter does not immobilize merely one fleeting state of the external world; through subtle means of his own, he seeks to express also the preceding state and that certain or likely to follow. His painting, therefore, contains potential movement, no longer expressed in space or in time, but in two-dimensional forms and in color. And that is why the forms and colors must be fictitious.

We have been questioning the role that painting plays in dramatic art. Now we are beginning to see that it is an indirect, though nonetheless rather important, one. *The work of the painter determines—and makes us aware of—the limitations that mobility forces upon us.* We see ourselves forced to forego the perfection and the completeness that immobility alone can guarantee; and if, deluding ourselves, we immobilize the play of the actors for even a moment, we sacrifice movement without receiving the least compensation. That is why a "living picture" is always distasteful to an artist, for it presents a fixed image of movement without its context.

And sculpture? It shares with painting the power to fix and immobilize a *chosen* instant of movement, and doubtless surpasses painting in the power to express the context of this movement. Like painting, then, it can depict a chosen moment and has certain qualities of perfection and completeness. But it is denied the infinite diversity of *fictitious* light, shadow, and color that painting can utilize. In compensation, it has plasticity —which calls forth living light. A tremendous compensation indeed! From our present standpoint, sculpture would appear to be of all others the most important single art, since its subject

· 11

is the human body.* The only thing that sculpture lacks is life, and therefore movement, which it must sacrifice to its perfection; but that is its only sacrifice. Obviously, a painted statue like those of the Greeks bears no relation to painting; this is mere coloring, not painting at all. Sculpture has nothing in common with painting.

Architecture is plastic; like sculpture, it calls forth living light, and it can be colored. In these respects it is of the same general order as sculpture. The fresco, the highest expression of painting and perhaps its only legitimate form, need not delude us; by the mere act of offering up plane surfaces to be painted, architecture does not assume thereby an organic relation to painting. The lines and reliefs of a structure merely furnish a framework for the painted fictions, and can bring out their fullest value only by remaining in absolute contrast with them. We all know what bad taste is displayed by paintings which attempt to deceive the eye by continuing or extending architectural lines or architectural perspective. They are like music played before a picture, in the vain hope that each will fully identify itself with the other; or like any other naive juxtaposition of unrelated aesthetic elements. Architecture is the art of grouping masses in relation to their weight; weight is its aesthetic principle. To express weight in a harmonious arrangement, measured by the scale of the living body and designed as a background for the mobility of that body: such is architecture's highest aim.

Gothic architecture expresses the weight of stone, by denying that weight. It thereby exerts a moral effort, but it appears in many places where that denial has no meaning and is therefore superfluous. What would we say of a ballroom or a theatre in Gothic style? Furthermore, a Gothic building made of wood or cardboard would be a monstrosity, since its triumph over weight—the only possible justification for an essentially misguided style—would no longer be expressed by the material

---

*Every other subject in sculpture grows out of architecture—of which it is then an ornament. The sculptor of animals is only a derived form of the sculptor of human beings; though the former's work is remarkable, it is not to be compared with the latter's.

12 ·

used in its construction. It is painful even to think of such a structure.* This art of weight, organically related to the human body and existing only for that body, is developed in space; without the presence of the human body, it remains inarticulate. Preeminently an art of space, architecture is conceived for the mobility of the living being. As we have seen, movement is the reconciling principle that formally unites space and time. Architecture is therefore an art which potentially embraces both time and space.

We have noted a characteristically fixed quality, as well as a characteristic achievement, in each of our arts, and have classed them as either arts of time or arts of space. We have found movement to be the sole reconciling factor between the two classes, since it fuses space and time into a single unit of expression. The living and mobile human body represents this reconciling element on the stage, and on this account is of primary importance. Its plasticity gives it close kinship with architecture and sculpture, but distinctly alienates it from painting. We have seen further that plasticity calls forth the real, inner life of light, while painting is but a fictitious representation of light.

Accepting these points, let us sum them up with somewhat more specialized attention to the so-called fine arts, the arts of space. All these—painting, sculpture, and architecture—are immobile; they evade time, so to speak. Painting, not being plastic, evades space as well, and therefore real and living light. It finds compensation for these great sacrifices in its power to evoke space in a chosen fiction; and its technique allows it to fix in this evocation an almost unlimited number of objects and to suggest the context of the instant it has chosen to immobilize. Its bearing on the idea of time-duration is, in a way, symbolic.

Sculpture is plastic; living in space, it therefore participates in living light. Like painting, it can suggest the context of chosen movements it is immobilizing, though it exists and acts as

---

*Constructions in iron are only indirectly governed by the law of weight; hence they rise only indirectly out of the special aesthetics of architecture.

a material reality rather than as a fictitious symbol.

Architecture is the art of creating fixed and circumscribed spaces, planned as a background for the presence and the movements of the living body. It expresses this purpose by its height, depth, and weight, and by the effect of its solidity. It is a realistic art; in architecture, the use of fictions is a luxury. By definition, it embraces space; in its practical applications, it embraces time as well. It is consequently the most richly endowed of all the fine arts.

We have just analyzed the three elements which the actor holds in one of his hands: the three static arts, the arts of space. Let us now seek to clarify in a similar way the arts of time—those of the poetical text and of music—which the actor holds in his other hand and which he is irresistibly compelled to unite with the arts of space.

It must be remembered here that in examining the text and the musical score from the point of view of the *mise en scène*, we are not entering into a discussion—for the moment, at least —of dramatic, literary, or musical composition, as such.

Leaving space, with or without implications of time relationships, behind us for the moment, we are here concerned with time itself. The idealized and arbitrary nature of our conception of time is too well known to require review. Let us merely note that this ideality of time is clearly asserted in art. Just as a long dream may take up but five minutes and thus may include a time-duration all out of proportion to that of normal time, so the time arts make use of normal time only as a kind of frame of reference for their special time-durations. During the dream, we accept its time-duration as natural, just as we accept the time-duration of the text or the music of a play. We should not think of consulting our watches; we should feel that they were lying!

The time arts, having time under their control, adapt it freely to their purposes. Not so with space and the space arts: our body, with its limited dimensions and capacities, and our eyes, with their limited faculties, settle that question. A painting that forced us to board a train in order to follow it out into space is unthinkable. However gigantic a sculptured figure may be, it preserves, after all, our relative proportions, and our eyes transpose these automatically. Nevertheless, such proportions, like those of a painting, are dependent on the potential limits of our vision.* An architecture that overreaches a scale applicable to the body's presence always violates its artistic function, and in extreme cases abandons this altogether. Unfortunately, examples of the latter type are only too numerous, and it is important for us to recognize the fact. Civilizations that have admitted the colossal in architecture are never those of a truly artistic people, a people whose art is *living*.

Why, then, has time no standard of measurement common to our waking life and our arts? Precisely because of its ideality. Time is ourselves. The arts that appeal to the eye are equally ourselves, in a sense, but they exist in space; and space has no ideality—our vision is too limited for that. Even though our hearing, too, has its limitations as to the duration of a work of art *measured by normal time,* yet it can occasionally adopt an imaginary time more or less disproportionate to the normal one. Struck by sound waves, our hearing apparatus transmits them to us *directly,* without any intermediate operation. In this matter, where other arts *employ symbolic reference,* that is, reach our emotions only through visual signs, music *is.* Such signs as it uses are inherently identified with its direct operation. It is the very voice of our soul; its ideality in time is therefore fundamental and legitimate.

But in regard to the *mise en scène* the heart of the matter is this: how can music be related to space? As we have seen, mobility expresses space by a succession of movements and hence by a succession of time-units. Thus mobility is found to be the intermediary element indispensable to the presence of the time arts on the stage. And, since there is reciprocity here, the space

*The sculptor's term "larger than nature" has nothing to do with the artistic quality of the work.

arts—thanks to the arts of time—can be expressed as units of time which would otherwise have been alien to them. They will thus indirectly share time's ideality.

Before examining how mobility can take its place in a work of art—and the question is of prime importance—it remains for us to consider, after discussing the art of sound and rhythm, the art of speech or of declamation.* In certain cases, the tone of the speaking voice can suggest an analogy to musical sound; in art, however, these two have absolutely nothing in common. A speaking tone differs from a musical one in that it is only an *intermediary* between the meaning of words and their significance in the brain; musical sounds, on the other hand, strike our emotions *directly*, and reasoning is a secondary operation in this case, if indeed it is necessary at all. Words whose meaning we do not know are merely more or less agreeable noises, not musical tones. As we begin to understand a foreign language, these noises take on significance; their physical vibrations progressively affect our understanding until we come to look upon them in a new way. They are *indirect* bearers of thought; musical tones are *direct* bearers of feeling.

Words express the ideality of time only in a limited and rudimentary way, and one that is completely dependent on our mental faculties. If a phrase is pronounced too rapidly, our minds cannot grasp it; and again, if it is drawn out too slowly, it loses its power to convey significance. If speaking tones and musical tones had not the element of time in common, they would be, aesthetically speaking, completely dissimilar. And even insofar as time is concerned, how are we to measure the varied time-durations of the spoken word with any degree of precision and certainty? Have we graphic signs by which we can indicate the time element in speech? Had the author diligently set down his intentions in this regard in the margins of this work—intentions which, through written signs, are after all addressed only to the

---

*Declamation, not reading. All reading is an outgrowth of literature, as such. An actor who reads or sings from a manuscript on the stage is only a reader or singer who is pointlessly misplaced.

16 ·

understanding—could they have had the precision indispensable to a work of art? Never! And for that reason the few traces of ideality that do exist in the time-durations of the spoken word are illusory.

In conclusion let us state that though speech is expressed in time, it cannot create, within the framework of normal time, any new and idealized time of its own. Only in superficial appearance, then, does it concern art in this matter of time; actually it is akin to art merely through the meaning of the words and through the arrangement necessary for their comprehension, if we leave aside for the moment the beauty that may result from the process. And it is only through this intelligible arrangement of words that a script becomes a work of art; it has no legitimate authority over the mobility of the human body. Its role is only indirect: transmitted by words to the emotions of the actor, the text gives over to the actor the entire responsibility for its realization in space.

These ideas, though they may appear obscure or paradoxical, are really of vital importance to a correct understanding of values in regard to the *mise en scène*. And I must repeat once again that this inquiry is undertaken from that point of view alone.

Let us return to music. Musical sounds have in themselves no meaning which can dictate their arrangement; their grouping is a spontaneous outgrowth of the musician's emotion. The abstract notations on the leaves of the score do not indicate the meaning of these sounds, but merely their arrangement—mathematically fixed both as to time-duration and to intensity. And this time-duration is directly dependent on the emotional sensibilities of the musician, without first passing through his understanding. Hence, the musician's feelings, his degree of sensitivity, create musical time-durations. Our feelings, as we already know, are independent of normal time: hence the musician is creating an unreal and idealized time *contained within* the normal one, but still aesthetically independent of it; and he has the almost miraculous power of precisely fixing his creation, this fictitious time. As a result, the time-durations of his music and those of his feelings are identical: his is an actual time, since it has duration, but it is also unreal. Aesthetically speaking, the reality of music is therefore greater than that of any of the other arts; it alone is a direct and spontaneous creation of our soul.

It might be held that the execution of music serves as an intermediary between it and ourselves. This is not true. The correct rendition of a musical score is to music what appropriate placing and lighting, for example, are to a fresco. Music *represents time;* it is its own intermediary. That is its formal function, particularly in regard to dramatic art. Music *is* the direct expression of our inner being; that is, its hidden life.

The dangerous theory that dramatic art can result from a mere combination of all the arts has in the past led us to analyze each one of them from that point of view, and from that point of view only. We can now catch a glimpse of the work there is left for us to do. To be organically unified—and therefore mutually subordinated—what sacrifices must the arts agree to? On the other hand, what compensations will they offer us, in their new mode of existence?

2. LIVING TIME

"WHEN MUSIC REACHES its noblest power it becomes form in space."[1]

More than a century has gone by since Schiller challenged the world with this prophetic message; and one may well ask how many of his contemporaries ever understood it. Did he himself fully grasp the implications of his statement? Was it not rather a flash of intuition than the decision of a reflective mind? It was probably the study of ancient art which impelled him—like a visionary—to this extreme. He began, perhaps, by *seeing* a rhapsodist in the ardor of mimetic improvisation—or did he visualize in his imagination some religious or dramatic ceremony of ancient Greece? How could he have found the basis for such a conclusion in the petty and conventional life of a German state in his day?

Schiller says merely "form in space." He does not elaborate; his vision reveals the incomplete and enigmatic character common to all prophecy. Who knows? Maybe the contemplation of an engraving of the Parthenon inspired him: his glance moved rhythmically from pillar to pillar; he saw in the frieze and the pediment an ultimate order, a harmony fixed there forever. Lowering his glance, perhaps he sensed that the weight of the upper structure rested directly on the flagstones of the temple, on a foundation of worn and real pillars . . . And perhaps a voice murmured, "Is this temple empty?"

But behold, a procession of celebrants climbs the steps

[1 Appia is apparently quoting from Schiller's *Uber die Aesthetische Erziehung des Menschen, in einer Reihe von Briefe*, the 22nd Letter: "Die Musik in ihrer höchsten Veredlung muss Gestalt werden und mit ruhigen Macht der Antiken auf uns wirken; . . ." He has added "in space."]

of the Acropolis. It draws nearer to the columns—and to the poet. The bare feet take hold upon the steps; the bodies, their form revealed by the folds of the tunics, are measured by the scale of the fluted columns. Would Schiller have understood? Next, he must have moved to the terraced auditorium of the theatre, and tried to imagine the evolutions of the chorus. Here the space about the altar is free and bare; no more friendly columns, revealing landmarks . . . How, then, can we know, measure and appreciate the changing proportions, which seem to elude us even as we begin to discover them? Once outside the temple, was he in the realm of the arbitrary, with no possibility of orientation?

It was, I am convinced, the burning desire to comprehend the incomprehensible relation between sounds and forms; to grasp the divine and fleeting spark lit by their very contact; to experience the inconceivable delight that the realization of their relation brings—it was this desire that compelled the great visionary to make such an affirmation, justified, as it was, by nothing in the life about him. He bequeathed to us his desire and his appeal: at last we are fortunate enough to be able to reply to him.

No! The proportions and the lines of the temple are not the arbitrary causes of joyous or solemn moods; the steps of the Acropolis do not prescribe a course for the naked feet; in the free space about the altar of the theatre, the chorus does not dance to an arbitrary rhythm . . . An ever-present and all-powerful principle is at work there; space itself must submit to its dictates. It was this principle that built the temple, proportioning its pillars and its steps. Invisible, it speaks to visible space; it animates forms, it develops lines. Its interpreter is the human body—the living, mobile body; from this body it has absorbed its life. This principle is *living;* through life, it becomes a regulating force; its language, understood by the body, is transmitted, vibrantly, to everything around it.

"When music reaches its noblest power, it becomes form in space."

Inanimate matter, the ground, the stones, do not hear the sounds; but the living body hears them!

The better one can obey, the better he can command. Mutual subordination will always remain the only substantial guarantee of the success of a collaboration. Subordination implies analysis; what am I to receive, and what must I give in return? A more or less willing neglect of this preliminary analysis lies at the root of most social and aesthetic errors. Devotion that only gives—and never takes—is misplaced devotion. The egotist wishes to conserve his riches for himself alone; his motive is often a noble one: he may be accumulating his treasure so that he may have more to offer later on. Yet the direction of his gesture remains the same; and his contribution to the partnership is never made.

If music hopes to regulate the mobility of the body, it must first learn what the body expects from it. Then it will ask itself questions, and seek to develop the faculty that is required; but this development, in turn, will be dependent on what the body will be able to offer the music. Unless music first receives life, it can give nothing living to the body. That is obvious. Hence, the body must deliver up its own life to the music, only to receive it anew, regulated and transfigured.

The varying lengths of musical sounds are realized in visible proportions in space. If music had but one sound and but one duration for this sound, it would remain time's slave; as it happens, however, it has a kinship with space. Through *groupings* of sounds. The variable time-durations of these groupings are capable of an infinite number of combinations; accordingly, they are responsible for the phenomenon of rhythm, which is not only akin to space, but can be fused with it, through movement. And the body is the bearer of movement.

The body behaves at the command of material necessity. But the feelings of the soul, too, are reflected in space—through gesture. Gestures, however, do not express the life of our soul directly. Their varying intensity and their varying length bear a very indirect relation indeed to the inner and hidden life of the soul. We can suffer for hours, and *indicate* it by a gesture of only a second's duration. Gesture in our daily life is a sign, a symbol, nothing more. Actors know this, and guide their acting by the very inconsistency between these two patterns of time-duration: that is, between that of the inner life of our soul and that of our physical body—the latter of which is certainly different from the former. Consequently, we live differently in time than in space; and the resulting conflict inevitably weakens our entire being in all its manifestations. Perhaps we would remain living enigmas on this account, if we did not possess—in music—the supreme corrective and regulator, springing directly from our affective life, and expressing it without any control other than that of our emotions.

Units of time in music correspond to those in our inner life; both are incompatible with the timing of our daily gestures. In this fact we reach the heart of the problem of living time; if previously I named music the supreme corrective and regulator, it was in anticipation of this point.

Let us proclaim here and now that, unless music is willing to deny its very nature, it must preserve those proportions in time which are characteristic of its existence. In this respect, actualism in dramatic art, as well as in pantomime, is a coarse negation of musical life.

If the body should modify the proportions and the duration of its gestures, would it necessarily suppress its inner nature and its inner life? Obviously not. For example, gymnastics—in order to strengthen our organism—impose on the body gestures whose proportions do not occur in our daily and natural life; but gymnastics do not necessarily suppress the life of our body thereby. In this simple technical exercise, we express the life of our body in a particular way, that is all. In music, on the contrary, a technical exercise is not music at all and its proportions do not concern us. The difference may seem subtle; but it is nonetheless evident, for we are treating of *life,* here.

Our body has movement under its control—any movement; and movement is the sign of life. On the other hand, music holds time under its control—but not *all* time. Music is the very expression of our soul. There is no parallel between the normal action of the body and the positive life of music. If such a parallel existed, our problems would be solved in advance; the union with music would take care of itself automatically. Such is not the case, and the solution is still to be found.

From the preceding, we can note which manifestations of the body possess the most independence, and which will have to be guided—docilely and compliantly—by the proportions of music. And one can conclude therefrom—strange as it may seem—that our body, in order to be put to the service of expressing our inner life—in order to express it, instead of merely referring to it symbolically—must modify its normal life considerably. But in undergoing such changes, will it not lose all its normal values? Is so profound a modification to be desired, and will the result be worth the sacrifice?

The reply to these questions is found in the principle underlying all art. Taine has put it, authoritatively and most definitely, into these words: "*The aim of a work of art is to reveal some essential, salient character, consequently some important idea, more clearly and more completely than can real objects. It achieves this through a group of parts whose relationships it systematically modifies.*"[1] The peculiar quality of art, then, lies in its modification of natural values. A painter who copies nature merely transposes it to a plane surface by means of color. If a sculptor copies his model, he is merely transposing, and like the painter, he is impoverishing nature.

The architect seems to fare better: he has nothing to copy. His work in itself is already a modification of natural forms; but if it loses sight of the proportions of the human body and of the diversified movements of life, its modifications are arbitrary and unjustifiable. The time arts, having nothing to copy, share the lot of architecture; they are still more closely related through their common kinship with the living being. One could almost

[1H. Taine, *Philosophie de L'art*, 2 vols. (Paris, 1881), I, 41-42.]

name poetry, music, and architecture in the same breath. The poet modifies the form and the time-duration of our daily thoughts; and the musician, as we have seen, modifies the time-durations of our normal life. Music would be highly arbitrary, if our affective life did not constantly regulate and justify it.

The human body, if it voluntarily accepts the modifications that music demands, assumes the rank of a means-of-expression in art; it forsakes its life of caprice and of accident so that it may express, under the control of music, some essential characteristic, some important idea, more clearly and fully than in normal life.

Schopenhauer, the philosopher-artist, assures us that "music never expresses the phenomenon, but only the inner essence of the phenomenon."[1] His conviction, put in this compact form, is like that of Taine; for it is very obvious that the essence of a phenomenon is clothed in a different form than that of the phenomenon itself.

Living time, then, will be the art of expressing an essential idea simultaneously in time and in space. Living time succeeds therein by making a succession of living forms of the human body and a succession of musical time-units mutually *solidary.*

[1 "... da sie nie die Erscheinung, sondern allein das innere Wesen. das Ansich aller Erscheinung, den Willen selbst, ausspricht." *Artur Schopenhauers sämtliche Werk: Erster Band, Die Welt als Wille und Vorstellung,* Paul Deussen, ed. (Munich, 1911), p. 308.]

3. LIVING SPACE

THUS FAR we have been chiefly concerned with music and with the living body. We touched upon the idea of space only through our discussion of bodily movements and of their regulation by means of musical time-units. But now these movements are going to be developed in the space which surrounds them, the atmosphere which envelopes them, and are going to seek allies in both.

The body is the interpreter of music for inanimate and inarticulate forms. Hence we can momentarily disregard music; the body, having absorbed it and being able to represent it in space, can guide us henceforth.

The body reclining, seated, or standing expresses itself in space by the movements of the arms, combined with the more limited ones of the torso and the head. Even when stationary, the legs maintain an appearance of mobility; their normal function, however, is to make actual movements in space. From the first, then, we can distinguish two types of planes: planes intended for movement, faster or slower, as the case may be, and subject to interruption; and those which exclude movement, serving to heighten the general effect of the body. These two types obviously overlap; only the moving presence of the body can determine to which class any single example belongs. For example, inclined planes, and especially stairways, could be considered participants in both types. However, the obstacle they offer to free movement and the expression they thereby give rise to in the organism are derived from the vertical plane.

We shall have to reckon, then, with two planes: first, the horizontal, for before all else, the body must rest on a plane, and in so resting must express its weight; and second, the vertical, which, corresponding to the upright body, accompanies it. The structure of the ground-plane—which is derived from the horizontal—must never lose sight of weight, but must seek to express it as clearly and as simply as possible.

Let me explain: The different pieces of furniture built for the comfort and rest of our body are so constructed that they weaken the contact which we make with non-living matter. We have springs, padding, and curved lines to embrace the human form; we round off corners, and soften hard surfaces with fabrics that silence noises and muffle contacts. We extend this weakening of the simple plane, as it were, so far that the expression of our movements is itself profoundly weakened thereby. Completely undressing oneself in a well-furnished room is convincing enough: our body without a mask, without the intermediary of the clothing, suddenly becomes a stranger to its surroundings. It becomes indecent in the etymological sense of the word—that is to say, out of place—and its expression borders on obscenity.

But, shall we say, a woman dressed becomingly and elegantly settled in an armchair is pleasantly expressive . . . Doubtless she is; but let her undress and seat herself in the same fashion on the same seat.

A bathroom with tapestries, couches, and cushions summons forth ideas incompatible with the true expressiveness of the body; while, if the same room offers only smooth and rigid surfaces as a background for the living body, the latter seems really present, and is enhanced aesthetically. Nude feet climbing a carpet-covered stair will be merely feet that are uncovered, and one wonders why. On an uncarpeted stair, they will be simply and expressively naked. Obviously, the feet of Mohammedans on the carpet of their mosques are merely uncovered rather than naked; they express a religious and not an aesthetic intention. But go outside the mosque and notice the nude feet of a woman descending the steps of the fountain; her feet will be gloriously naked . . .

Anything that tends to alter the expression of weight, no

matter what purpose it serves, weakens bodily expression. Hence the first principle of *living* art—perhaps the one from which all others are consequently and automatically derived—must be: all inanimate forms must *oppose* rather than embrace all living forms. If there are times when flexibility of line is desirable in order to weaken the expression of a movement or an attitude momentarily, then the flexibility itself—because of that accomplishment—becomes momentarily expressive. However, if this procedure is prolonged, the positive presence of the body will be nullified to an ever-increasing degree. The body will be present, but without bodily effect; its movements will become superfluous and therefore ridiculous, or will be reduced to symbols. In that case, we shall be falling back into daily life—or into a theatre of manners.

We have seen that in architecture, too, weight is a factor that is absolutely indispensable to bodily expression. Weight, not mere heaviness! Weight is a principle. Through it, matter asserts itself; and the thousand steps in this assertion make up its expression. Volume without weight seems about to escape into the breeze, like a balloon; its stability is illusory; it is a portion of space momentarily enclosed, nothing more. Volume is like an inflated rubber doll, and for this reason the ballet dancer resembles a captive balloon, brought back at regular intervals to its moorings. To receive its portion of life from the living body, space must oppose this body; space that embraces our body only further augments its own inertness. But opposition to the body gives life to the inanimate forms of space. *Living* space is the victory of bodily forms over inanimate forms. The mutuality is complete.

We sense this opposition in two ways: either through the contrast in lines when we look at someone else's body in contact with rigid forms in space; or else when our own body verifies the resistance with which these forms oppose it. The first is only a secondary proof; the other is a personal—and therefore decisive—experience.

For example, let us imagine a square, vertical column,

with sharply-defined angles. This column rests, with no base, on horizontal slabs. It gives an impression of solidity, of power to resist. A body approaches. Out of the contrast between its movement and the quiet immobility of the column is born a sensation of expressive life, a sensation that the body without the column or the column without the advancing body could not have evoked. Further, the sinuous and rounded lines of the body differ essentially from the plane surfaces and the angles of the column— and this contrast is in itself expressive. The body finally touches the column; the opposition is further accentuated. Finally the body leans against the column, and the latter's immobility offers a point of solid support: the column resists; it *acts!* The opposition has created life in the inanimate form; the space has become living!

Let us suppose now that the column is rigid only in appearance, and that its material, at the slightest pressure from without, would embrace the form of the body touching it. In that case the living body would be incrusted in the soft material of the column; its life would be entombed; at the same time it would take away the life of the column. (*Sofas deep as the tomb.* Baudelaire.)[1] The point is too obvious to require further examples. The ground itself affords a similar experience. Take as an example an elastic ground-surface, which would allow the foot to sink in at each step, but, when the foot had been removed, would at once resume its former shape. This ground would move, in a sense; but would its mobility be living? Let us look at the surface restored behind the steps of the living body: it is expectant, only waiting to give way again. Opposing nothing, it is dead; nothing could be more lifeless. And the feet that press it down encounter no resistance; the play of the muscles is deadened in a literal sense of the word. If one continued to walk across such a surface, he would finally lose all feeling for spontaneous movement, he would be ready to accept a mechanism which, raising one foot after the other, drives them forward. In that case both

---

[1"Des divans profonds comme des tombeaux," Charles Baudelaire, "La Mort des Amants" in *Les Fleurs du Mal*.]

28 ·

the ground and the body would be mechanical, a condition that is a supreme negation of life and the beginning of the ridiculous. (See Bergson.)[1]

And now let this negative ground, which is always ready to give way, be transformed into rigid slabs, which, on the contrary, await the foot only to resist it, to throw it back at each new step, and to prepare it for a new resistance; through its rigidity, such a surface involves the entire organism in the spontaneity of walking. By opposing itself to life, the ground, like the pillar, can receive life from the body.

Hence the principles of weight and solidity are indeed primary considerations in the existence of a *living* space. These principles would seem to allow us a more or less free choice of line. Since the body possesses a definite structure, we can modify it in space only by modifying its movements. But the choice of lines in space—although they must always oppose those of the body—would seem, in general, to be up to us; that privilege would be a compensation for their immobility, as is the case in the fine arts. It might seem to us, then, that after taking account of weight and solidity, we have a free field, and, like other artists, can choose and can be as subtle as we wish in our aims and our creations.

But in that case we are forgetting that we are not—like the sculptor or the painter—alone before a lump of clay or a section of a wall that is to be decorated: we are working with a living body. With it alone are we concerned in space; to it alone do we give orders; by it and through it alone can we relate ourselves to inanimate forms. Without it, all our experiments would be fruitless and stillborn. In the hierarchy of living art, the place for our creative imagination is between time and the living and mobile body; that is, between the music that we compose and the body that must be pervaded by and must embody this music. In this sense, we precede the body. But afterwards, the body speaks; we become merely its interpreter, and can create nothing in our own right. Only our confident and conscious submission

[1]Henri Bergson, *Le Rire; essai sur la signification du comique* (Paris, 1900).]

to music—the expression of our inner life—has brought us the power to dominate the living body. And the body, in turn, through its complete submission to our call, wins the right to regulate the space surrounding and touching it: *directly*, we are incapable of such regulation.

This hierarchial phenomenon is most interesting; it is because we have not verified and obeyed its laws that our scenic and dramatic art are so completely confused.

The friendly reader who has followed me this far may have noticed that, little by little, I am allowing music to take preference over the spoken text; and perhaps he is astonished or offended. For clarity in exposition, however, I must still continue this apparent violence, and postpone a little longer an explanation of my motives. Therefore, let us consider only music for the moment, and let us once more establish the following hierarchy; music imposes its successive units of time on the movements of the body; this body, in turn, interprets them in terms of space. Inanimate forms, by opposing their solidity to the body, affirm their own existence—which, without this opposition, they cannot manifest so clearly—and thus close the cycle; beyond that, there is nothing. In this hierarchy, we possess only a musical text, beyond which all the rest follows automatically by means of the human body.

For our eyes, then, *living* space—thanks to the intermediary of the body—will be the resonator for the music, so to speak. One could even advance the paradox that inanimate spatial forms, to become *living*, must obey the laws of a visual acoustics.

4. LIVING COLOR

W E COULD have named this chapter living light, but that would have been tautology. Light is to space what sounds are to time—the perfect expression of life. For the same reason, we did not need to speak of living music, but only of a musical time that can be translated into space. Color, on the contrary, is a derivative of light; it is dependent thereon, and—from the scenic point of view—dependent in two distinct ways. Either the light takes possession of and becomes one with the color, in order to diffuse it in space, in which case the color shares the existence of the light itself; or the light is content to illuminate a colored surface of an object, in which case the color remains attached to that object, receiving life only by virtue of the object, and through variations in the light which makes it visible.

Color, in the first instance, is ambient, pervading the atmosphere, and—like the light—taking part in movement; consequently, it bears a direct and intimate relation to the human body. In the second, color can act only by opposition and reflection; if it moves at all, it does not move of itself, but only with the object which reflects it. Therefore, though its life is not fictitious, as in painting, yet it is totally dependent. A red tapestry, brusquely pushed aside, is involved in a movement; but it is not the red color that moves—it is the tapestry, from which the color is inseparable. The same quantity of the same color, hung on the panel of a door, would follow the passive and clumsy movement of the door. Such an effect with a moving tapestry—often an important one—is the result of the flexibility of the colored material, and not essentially of that of the color itself.

· 31

These distinctions are necessary for the correct handling of color in *living* space; they prove the difference existing between color in painting—a fiction on a plane surface—and color in action, effectively diffused in space.

This leads us to the inevitable principles of sacrifice and compensation. We already know the important advantages that the painter finds in the immobility of his work. But so far we have observed the nature neither of the sacrifices imposed on scenic (and dramatic) art by mobility, nor of the possible compensations. In the first place, there is no question here of picking a special instant — a chosen instant — as the painter and the sculptor do; movement is a succession of details. We can choose the succession, but we cannot stop it at a precise moment. (See p. 21 on the subject of the living picture.) Selecting a precise moment, the painter fixes the context of the gesture that he chooses; on the contrary, if one interrupts a succession of movements, the attitude that is immobilized is the result of the preceding movement, and the preparation for the one that is to follow. But it only holds them in check; it does not express them effectively, as a painting can do. This interruption is arbitrary; its character is accidental; because of it, movement wanders for a moment from the domain of art.

Now, it is this very principle of immobility which gives painting its finished character, its perfection; and since *living* art must renounce this perfection, the sacrifice is quite apparent —especially in the case of color. If movement were to become purely mechanical, one could, with difficulty, imagine a fixation of the elements of expression minute enough so that it could aspire to something like perfection. But the sacrifice in that case would be to renounce art, for which nothing could compensate. Nevertheless, there are great artists who, by the same path we have just traveled, have arrived at the choice of marionettes— and have adopted them. Their desire to be found *alone* in front of the stage, like the painter in his workshop, has prevailed! Such a choice is perhaps excusable. But how can we imagine a living, corporeal humanity content in the long run with a dramatic art that is mechanized? Would that not oblige us to be still more passive in the theatre than we already are? Or would these artists wish to demand that we—their spectators—continually *animate* their characters for them? Such an activity on our part would have nothing at all in common with that which every work of art requires of us. Dramatic art is above all an art of life; and it is precisely in relation to the representation of that life, given as a point-of-departure, that we must effect a synthesis.

It is salutary for us to be exposed to such a wholly deceptive logic, and to breathe in its deadly miasmas. As a result, we only aspire more earnestly to the bracing atmosphere of art, and submit thereafter—knowingly and willingly—to its austere discipline. In art, logic is life; the reverse is not true. We can present life; we can never comprehend it. And if the artist of genius stands before his finished work as he would before a mystery—a mystery for its creator—that is because he has given us—unaware—the meaning of life in a symbol. But he feels it; he almost understands it—and we do, too!

A mechanical art would be like an automobile, which puts time and space at our disposal, but does not express them. The artist, in offering us only a symbol, convinces us of both our mysterious power and our limitations: he *modifies* our passionate desire to know, and creates thereby a work of art whose existence can transfigure the walls that close us in. He does not deny the existence of these walls, but he makes them transparent: with him, we touch the obstacle, yet we penetrate it.

All this on the subject of color? Yes; the sacrifice that scenic art must make in relation to painting is one of the most perceptible—and for most people, the most difficult—that the new order of things will require. It demands a profound change in our customary notions and desires; only the most weighty arguments in its favor will be effective.

In analyzing the essential character of painting, we saw that it has nothing in common with living space and living time.

It is only proper, then, to distinguish clearly the idea of painting —fictitious groupings of colors—from the idea of color in itself. Therein Taine's "modification" finds its most radical application; for painting must renounce not only painting's inherent charm, but above all its unique power to represent an almost unlimited number of objects. Thus our loss in giving up painting is beyond the ordinary and presupposes a compensation proportionate to the sacrifice. But the least concession on the part of the creative artist would deny life to the new art; his revelation would be an illusion; he would re-cover our walls with tinsel, instead of penetrating them with light.

Now for the first time — apropos of painting — do we touch upon the very source of dramatic art. The elementary principles that we have put forth and defended up to this point could have been applied to dramatic art in the manner in which strict counterpoint is applied to free musical composition. We should have been able to violate them according to our taste, just as a painter occasionally modifies the proportions of the body to add to their effectiveness—on condition, of course, that he knows these proportions perfectly. As for painting, there is no choice for us; its essential principles are opposed to its use on the stage. Dramatic art is an art—in the strongest sense of the word—only when it renounces painting. *In the very conception of the art,* this renunciation is a question of life or death. But dramatic art is under obligation to replace, in some fashion or other, what we used to expect from a painted setting. Hence, the reform is concerned with even the drama itself. But before handling such reform from the general point of view we have reached in our investigations, we might make it more intelligible by means of examples and considerations of detail.

Do we wish to represent on the stage a countryside with certain of its people? If so, we can have a countryside—but one that is unrelated to the characters; there will be a countryside on one hand, characters on the other. If we wish a character or two *in* a definite countryside, we are faced with an impossibility: they will be *before* the painting, and not *within* it! Or do we seek

34 ·

a particular style of construction, a historically exact street? Such a street must be painted, for the most part, on vertical drops; and the actor will walk up and down *before* the painting, and not *in* the street. However, were it constructed and set up in three dimensions (a procedure that would be, in every conceivable case, a luxury disproportionate to the proposed end), then exact and correct architecture without solidity or weight would be put in contact with a living body possessing both.*

It will be the same with any setting the author may choose, if he does not start exclusively with the plastic and living body of the actor. It is from this body that the stage decoration must be born or must rise—and not from the detached imagination of the dramatist. We know now that only the living body of the actor can dictate to space . . .

Yet a dramatic action almost always contains some ideas that the text in itself is powerless to give us. Must we return to the signboard of the Shakespearean stage? That would not be so bad, after all. But certainly another more discreet and less incongruous means is to be found, for a written description, which is to be read by the spectators during the speeches of the actor, suggests a troublesome analogy; and such written words are decidedly far removed from the body in action. These ideas —with which we still burden the painted setting—need not *express* anything, but only *indicate* it, since a signboard formerly sufficed to orient the spectators.

Is there no place in the scenic scheme of things, we may well ask, for an element of indication, of orientation, independent of the hierarchy of *living* art—an element which, approximating the indications in the text, and seeming to grow out of the text, would yet involve space, directly and in its own right, without necessarily involving the actor? This element would be entirely distinct from the expressive elements depending on the

---

*One is reminded of the laborious effect which the counterfeit and ephemeral constructions of the great expositions produce, and how they tend to pervert both fine sensibilities and good taste.

· 35

actor alone; we could name it *indication* in contrast to *expression*, whose rank is strictly hierarchical. The "indication" would represent on the stage that portion of the text for which the actor cannot be responsible; visually, it would serve just as an oral description would serve, if the latter were taking the place of action. This element would function where the elements of expression—music, the body, space, light, and color—would be helpless. It would belong to the text, which signifies, but does not express; but it would be addressed to the eye.

By way of analogy and example, musical expression—unless it is made fruitful, so to speak, by the poet—remains in abstractions; dramatic art, which is concrete, would be embarrassed by abstractions. But the spoken text, by itself, fails in direct expression—which music alone can bring to it. Consequently, on one hand we have expression without "indication," without the necessary orientation; on the other, "indication" without expression. It is just the same with space. The sovereign expression which the music of the body accords to space must be made fruitful in dramatic art by some form of "indication." Our eyes, like our ears, demand orientation. So, if the elements of expression do not implicitly contain this intelligible "indication," and if the speeches fail, too, in this respect, then we must find it in space.

Painting, so to speak, *signifies* form, light, color, *etc.*, in a fiction like that of a poetical text without music; hence, it is qualified to take the role of visible symbolization whenever this is indispensable. Its role will be entirely dependent on the scenic hierarchy— to which, however, it will not belong. The elements of expression will use it only in urgent cases; and, just as a Shakespearean signboard did not give complete details of a countryside or of a building, so the pictorial "signification" will need to give only the barest suggestion. Using only what is absolutely necessary for a brief and yet immediate orientation, it will advantageously replace the signboard, that is all. In many cases, living light and living color will be able to approximate the "signification" by making their expression concrete through the form or the movement of a shadow, the color or the direction of a light.*

Fine distinctions are thus quite naturally weakened in the practical work of the dramatist and stage-director, but they are nonetheless indispensable if the elements of production are to be handled correctly. There is still another type of "indication," which (without actually having grown out of the text, and without serving as necessary orientation) is like the notations added to a musical score in order to insure the exact interpretation of the music. This type makes the expression precise without explaining it; by a visible symbol, it confirms the ideality of the place, and relates the living body to this symbol. Certain details of space, of fixed color used with fluctuations in light, of ambient color, of partial obstructions casting more or less mobile shadows which mean nothing definite, but which contribute to the life of the movement—are of this type. There is one condition, however: the living body must accept them as playing a part in its creation in space. The dramatist-stage-director is a painter whose palette should be *living;* his hand is guided in the choice of living colors, their mixture, their arrangement, by the actor. Then the actor himself is plunged into this light, realizing in time what the painter could conceive only in space.

By renouncing the fictitious role it has in painting, color attains life in space; but in that case it becomes dependent on light and on plastic forms, which determine its variable importance. Its *living* reality deprives it of the objects which it would represent fictitiously on the canvas; we need hardly seek its help, then, to represent objects on the stage. (There is an exception, as we have seen, in the case of the indications, the symbolizations, that are indispensable to the spectator's orientation.)

Living color is the negation of painted stage settings. For dramatic art, what will be the consequences of rejecting painted settings?

---

*A trellis, for example, can be clearly indicated merely by the pattern of the shadows that the light from above throws on the ground or on the walls; both the living body and inanimate forms will assist. This pattern, made by invisible obstructions, can even take part in the movement, if it itself moves, and thus creates moving shadows.

5. ORGANIC UNITY

W HEN A PAINTER seeks a subject, he bears in mind not
only the resources and advantages that the art form he
is using offers him, but also the restrictions and the sacrifices
that it imposes. He is ever conscious of both the possibilities
and the impossibilities in painting; he is so accustomed to them
that his life as a painter and the knowledge that there are certain
inevitable limitations in his art are identified, so to speak, in an
affirmation: He is a painter, and therefore he enjoys certain
advantages, must consent to certain sacrifices. As a result, he
experiments within these limitations, feeling that they are incon-
testable.

What about the dramatist? If he is truly a dramatist, all
his activity is in anticipation of the actual presentation of his
written work: he seeks to appeal not to readers, but to spectators.
Since a play is produced in a theatre but a manuscript is prepared
elsewhere, the dramatist is obliged to divide his attention between
a work whose master he is—the manuscript of his play—and a
process which usually escapes his control—the production of that
play. He oscillates between the two just as a painter would, if his
still empty canvas were already hung in an exhibition, while his
palette, covered with fresh colors, remained in his studio. At the
exhibition, he would vainly seek to conjure up the proper arrangement of colors; in his workshop he would eagerly wish for the
liberating surface of the canvas.

But the desire of a dramatist for a stage is less fixed and
less exact than that of a painter for a canvas. The dramatist's
palette can be running over with situations and can in a pinch
suffice; but he thus plays a lone and dangerous game, since his

palette concerns only half his work. The moment of the exhibition—that is, of the staging—has come. The author takes to the theatre the results of his thoughtful and concentrated labor. Has his canvas—the stage—the qualities and the dimensions he dreamed about in the silence of his workroom? Alas! no one attends to that! The stage is the stage, to take or to leave; the play is always the factor to be incommoded. The stage is never ready to concede: it is not made that way. The thing written on paper must always be elastic enough to adopt as unalterable whatever conditions are prescribed for it.

How happy is the lot of the painter! He can take his canvas into his studio, to unite it—as it were—with his palette; he can preside at their wedding in privacy. The dramatic author must take his manuscript to the theatre; in this case, the union is consummated not precisely in mystery and meditation — nor, above all, in silence! The two parties concerned, knowing each other only by hearsay, make some mutually strange discoveries. They are assured that this is the way things must be, always have been, and always will be. Accordingly, they are resigned, after a time. The bride—the stage—is dressed without regard to the taste of the groom—the drama, bullied, bruised, and even mutilated, ends by half disappearing in the gaudy dress of the bride. Then the guests are bidden to enter, and the festivity is in full swing—in the presence of the author of so much evil, who forgets his shame in the applause and the uproar. When this unhappy being returns to his work chamber, a little while ago so well filled with almost living people, he sees nothing now but a few daubed papers. If he returns to the stage, he can only wipe off the poisoned dust from still more bedaubed canvases. And if he lingers between the two, he feels his work escaping and eluding him forever. Such is the work of the dramatic author.

But let us come back to the artists who, like the painter, identify their existence with both the favorable and the restrictive requirements of their "profession," who would never harbor the idea of separating their highest artistic aspirations from the means of execution characteristic of their art. For a painter, the brush, the colors, and the plane surface that he uses are in a sense his way of thinking, his manner of conceiving his work; he knows these materials, and he seeks no further. It is the same with other artists. There is one, however, who is an exception: the artist without a name, of the art without a name . . .

The dramatic author never considers the stage, as it is offered to him, as definite technical material. He always agrees to accommodate himself to the stage; he even goes so far as to shape his artistic thought according to this sad model, and he does not suffer too much in the process, for this is apparently the only way he can achieve a minimum of harmony. His situation is like that of a painter who is allowed an insufficient number of colors, and a canvas of fixed but ridiculous dimensions. It is really worse than that, for a painter of genius will always find the means to express himself, as long as the essential principles of his technique are not perverted; that is to say, as long as he can work with brush, colors, and plane surface. But our modern stage offers the dramatist nonsensical technical material; it is not a medium which can be truly dedicated to dramatic work—only through an inconceivable outrage are we obliged to accept it, or even to consider it, as such a medium. Unfortunately, the habit is formed. It is with this material that we evoke dramatic works, and, what is worse, it is with this material that the dramatist conceives these works, fearing lest he be not "theatrical." The term is hallowed: it is never our stage that is accused of not being "theatrical," but always the dramatist himself. That is why he is an artist without a name: he does not dominate a technique; the technique of the stage dominates him. An artist must be free; the dramatist is enslaved. Today he is not—and cannot be—an artist.

One of the aims of this book is to support the dramatic author in his efforts to achieve the enviable rank of artist, a rank which he could merit. To this end, we must give him technical material that *belongs to him,* thereby setting him to work as an artist.

Slavery, like all other habits, can become second nature;

it has become that for the dramatist and for his public. This is a question of conversion, then, in the truest sense of the word. A function creates its organ. That in physiology or zoology this affirmation is only approximative, matters little here, for it is evident that in art it is profoundly correct. In our day, the function of the dramatist has not created its organ; that is, a work of dramatic art is not presented to our eyes *organically,* but through an artificial, exterior mechanism which does not belong to the dramatic organism. Hence, we must probably seek within the function itself the weak point which has placed the dramatist in dependence and which helps to keep him there.

We have already completed an analysis of the different arts from the sole point of view of the dramatic art, and independent of existing processes of staging; perhaps this analysis will aid us here. Should not the dramatist himself have suggested the principles of our stage decoration from the very beginning? And is he not now in danger of further postponing this initiating impulse through sheer inertia and blundering? The indiscriminate use of painting is so characteristic of all our staging that painted canvases and stage decoration are almost synonymous to us. Now, all artists know that the aim of these canvases is not to present an expressive combination of colors and forms, but to "indicate" — as we have seen above — a group of details and objects. We must suppose that a real need for showing us these objects accounts for the author's seeking help from the painter. The painter, of course, responds eagerly!

If we put ourselves in the place of the author at the moment he chooses his subject, it is evident that this is the precise moment in which his technical liberty or dependence is decided. If the author decides that he can free himself from the means imposed by the stage, he is immediately confronted by the necessity of determining *the essential nature of a subject intended for representation.* From his point of view, a subject is concerned with characters in conflict with one another; from this conflict arise particular circumstances that make the characters react; out of their way of reacting, dramatic interest is born. To a dramatic author, this is all; dramatic art, consisting entirely of such reactions, is apparently capable of infinite variety. But he soon perceives that such is not the case; that the reactions do not vary infinitely; on the contrary, they are repeated without change; that in this sense human nature is limited; and that each of our passions has a name. As a result, he seeks to vary the interest through diversity in character; and there begin his difficulties—difficulties of dimension. To present a character, one needs time on the stage, space on paper; thus the choice is limited. The novel and the psychological study have an indefinite space — on paper, of course—at their command; a play has but three or four hours.*

We must seek elsewhere for variety, then; here the influence of the setting comes into play. The setting is always geographical and historical, dependent on a climate and a culture which are indicated visually by a group of specific objects. Unless the audience can see these objects, the text of the play must convey a quantity of information that will completely paralyze the action. As a result, we are forced to represent them in the stage decoration.

There is more to the problem of stage decoration than the mere question of whether or not a setting can be executed. In the theatre we are not at the cinema; the laws that rule the stage are, above all, technical ones. To wish to represent nearly everything on the stage, and to invoke on that account the so-called liberty of the artist, is deliberately to lead dramatic art beyond its own limits and consequently beyond the domain of art. As long as an author remains content to show characters and their reactions, he finds himself relatively independent as far as his work is concerned. But from the moment when he uses the influence of the setting to vary his motifs, he meets with problems of staging, and must reckon with them. Under present conditions his only concern is the possibility of representing things on the stage. He will reject all projects that are too difficult to represent; in general, he

---

*To put on the stage a character whose description and development need a volume of 300 pages is one of the banal monstrosities of our theatre.

will confine his choice to places and things that he knows are easy to realize in production and are suitable for maintaining the illusion which is so dear to him. Like the ostrich, he chooses to ignore danger. But how can he help perceiving that decorative technique is regulated by laws other than those of possibility? If he has money to throw out of the window, an author can obtain anything on the stage. The Romans caused a river to pass through the Circus, in the midst of vegetation like that of a virgin forest. The Duke of Meiningen bought museums, apartments, and palaces in order to realize two or three scenes. The results in both cases were artistically regrettable.

No; stage decoration is regulated by the presence of the living body. This body is the final authority concerning the possibilities of realization; everything that is incongruous or inconsistent in relation to its presence is "impossible," and suppresses the play.

In the choice of his subject, the author must question, not the director-designer, but the actor. Such a generalization, of course, is not meant to suggest that he seek advice from this actor or from that. It is the Idea of the living actor — plastic and mobile—that must be his guide. For example, he must ask himself whether a certain setting is in keeping with the presence of the actor, and not merely whether its realization is "possible." From a technical point of view, his choice is concerned with the importance he wishes to—or must—give to the influence of the setting. From both points of view, he must choose with a full knowledge of conditions, and consequently must know perfectly the normal scenic hierarchy and its results.

His technique as an artist determines his choice. The painter is not irked by the fact that plastic relief is denied him; his technique simply does not permit such a possibility. So must it be for the dramatic author. He need not be distressed by the fact that he cannot place his character in a cathedral, but rather by the fact that he cannot free the character from conditions harmful to its full realization on the stage. The novelist and the epic poet can evoke their heroes by means of description; their

· 43

work is a story that is told, and the action is placed *in* the story, since it is not living. But the dramatic author is not merely telling a story; his living action is free, stripped of all drapery. Every indication of specific place tends to bring it nearer to the novel or the epic, and to remove it further from dramatic art. The more "indication" of place is necessary to the action—that is, to make the characters, the events, and the reactions plausible—the more the action will be estranged from *living* Art. *The reason is purely and simply a technical one, and no one can change it in any way.*

The more a painter approaches sculpture, the less he will be a painter; the more a sculptor seeks for ambience, the less he will be a sculptor. The less the dramatic author makes his characters dependent on the "indications" in the setting, the more he will be a dramatist. For when anyone says "Dramatist," he says "Stage-director" in the same breath; it is a sacrilege to specialize the two activities. We may set up as a rule, then, that if the dramatist does not insist on controlling both, he will be incapable of controlling either—since it is from their mutual correlation that *living* art must be born. Only in very rare exceptions do we yet have this supreme art or its artist. By misplacing the center of gravity, so to speak, we divide our art; in one respect our dramatic art rests on the author, in another on the director-designer. Sometimes it relies more on the one, sometimes on the other; it should rest simply and clearly on the dramatist himself.

The technical synthesis of the elements of representation finds its source in the *initial idea* of dramatic art. It depends on an *attitude* of the author. This attitude frees him; without it, he is not an artist.

Doubtless by this time the reader is wondering what this attitude, this initial idea, is, after all. Perhaps he feels what it is, and would like to know.

There is one question in art that is continually coming to the fore, continually provoking almost endless discussions. I refer to the question of a *Subject* for a work of art, and of the point up to which a work of art admits of a subject — a subject which requires a *title*.

In reality, every work of art supplies its own title; from a fresco, majestic and explicit in itself, to the most trifling improvisation on the piano. One might well believe that artists seriously doubt the import or the interest of their works, if one is to judge by their insistence on titles. Just as many pictures of festive gatherings or landscapes are apparently granted a semblance of the right to existence by their wretched and pretentious captions, so many rich and virile works are reduced to the level of simple illustrations by the addition of superfluous titles. In music, for example, a simple indication of the key and of the number and general class of the work gives an impression of nobility that a title can never achieve. The *Eroica* gains nothing by having a title; and it would be revolting to name the *Ninth Symphony* differently . . .

However (and this *however* is always a cause of tumultuous discussions), since the artists themselves generally title their works, have they not other motives for such a procedure, possibly, beyond that of doubt concerning the comprehension of the audience? Do artists need a definite stimulus to create certain works? There are profound thinkers who think only with pen in hand. In the case of artists, does the title take the place of a pen?

The problem, then, may be considered under two different aspects: concern in regard to the audience, and the need of a stimulus. We know with what care and ardor artists display their works; what importance they attach, in spite of everything, to criticism and to the rewards they find in fame. However, even if they do not disregard their public, they are still conscious of the abyss that separates them from that public—in our day, at least. And titles are doubtless a connecting link between artist and public: they answer the eternal question, "What does that represent?" This question is the first that the eyes of the visitor express when he looks at a work of art; only afterwards—and this next step is still the exception—does the onlooker little by little become a contemplator. When the visitor knows what the work is to represent, he deferentially adds the name of the artist; then,

· 45

calm and satisfied, he sets out to judge whether or not the work corresponds to the title.

No one would buy a catalogue without titles. A concert without a program would throw the listener into utter confusion. Why? Can he seriously contend that, if it is a symphony, he will be preparing for that symphony, and so on? Oh, no! But he maintains that, after reading about the piece in the program, he knows "what it is." Such knowledge glosses over his own passivity and indolence; and if by chance the title of the piece is suggestive, he is as comfortable as can be. Who has not seen the glance of curiosity and pleasure with which he runs over the program, and the vague and disinterested eyes he raises when he has finished? When he is too bored during a piece, he has new recourse to the program, and finds new comfort there. It seems to say: "Indeed, this is not merely sounds—here is the title." And for a moment he listens anew, less passively.

It could be held that except for the stimulation of going out for a change, of entering the concert hall, of settling in the seat, of looking and being looked at, of breathing the particular air of a crowded hall, of watching the performers at rest, of buying the program and being impressed with it, and so forth— without these the audience of the concert artist would get almost nothing. What a difference between the interested and glowing expression on the features of the audience as it is arriving and getting settled, and the one it assumes as soon as the music begins! This is the heart of the matter: the music asks for something. But the audience always forgets until it is too late; it has brought everything but that . . .

With a program in hand, the audience can judge the evening's offerings. Now, nothing in its being is ever able to react strongly, to participate joyously and courageously in the creation of the artist; consequently the audience must be oriented before-hand, so that it can search quickly among its memories or its feelings for something that corresponds to the title. If even then the audience finds nothing, the title adds still more to its trouble, and the work is doubly an enigma. Take, for example: "A Look into Infinity." Although the auditors—in the majority—have had these eternal and infinite words on their lips, they have never really mused over them. This symbol, which attempts to give the auditors something of the human essence, remains a closed book to them. It is useless for them to withdraw a little, with an intelligent air, or to blink their eyes: this shamming about a work whose very title escapes them, does not bring them closer to it. Moreover, this title shows, on the artist's part, either an error of judgment or a need of a stimulus—perhaps both.

It should be unnecessary to identify title with subject. We know from history, for example, that the lives of mighty heroes were the subjects imposed upon Egyptian artisan-sculptors and painters; again, that religious subjects were long the public justification for a work of art. This latter tendency was prolonged like a bad habit. Claude Lorrain gives biblical titles to his landscapes! In such a case, title and subject are tied together in order to express the culture, the particular temper of an age; the title answers no question. A beautiful woman with a child on her knees can be only a Madonna; if Raphael had called his painting "Peasant Woman of the Campagna," people would have cried out at the scandal.

Our modern culture has opened up all fields to us; there are so many subjects to choose from that for the artist it is a matter of anarchy rather than freedom. Art has no public now; the public, no art. Art has no direct concern with us any more, and for good reason; hence, we need to have works of art explained to us—works as strange to us as an exotic jewel whose form does not suggest its use. So far as he is concerned, the artist, not finding his work in us—in us, who should be his subject and his title—seeks it elsewhere. Elsewhere, subject and title are no longer closely identified; and his anarchical freedom quite naturally forces the artist to limit his conception cautiously, at the very moment of its birth. He therefore determines the conception by means of a title, and securely fastens himself to this fixed and intelligible point in the vexing sea of possibilities. The public takes the result in good faith, without too much suspicion that the title, in this case, is to the artist what the pen is to the thinker. It enabled the work to be developed, that is all; its worth is not intellectual, but moral. The artist needed it; but, his work finished, he retained it, foolishly enough — like a builder who would retain his scaffolding on a finished building.

To wish to represent a subject is always to forsake creating a work of art — which, in its essence, is pure and simple expression, with no regard to a given subject. To give a work a title is to acknowledge its quality as a mere explanation of something. To take a subject without titling it—even in one's inmost thoughts—is to tend toward a work of art. To achieve an "expression" that stems only from an irresistible desire, and has no precise object—this is to create a work of art. If one finds afterwards that he can give to that work of art a more or less specific and particular name, this is something else entirely, having nothing in common with mere explanation. On the contrary, it is proof of the reality of the artist's desire, and of its mysterious and profound humanity. If our art had a public, the titles of many works might, indeed, become objects of veneration, and might lead us to profound emotion, by introducing us to the most secret sanctuary of the artist, a sanctuary sometimes hidden even from him.

The foregoing discussion brings us to ideas of Indication and Expression; of the choice the dramatic author must make in relation to them; and of the *attitude* resulting from this choice. Like other artists, he finds himself torn between the desire to express something, and the need for Expression; between a subject to express, and an Expression to represent. By tending toward "indication" he makes himself responsible for intelligible ideas which seriously affect the stage setting—as we have seen—and which weaken the expression he desires. By tending toward Expression, however, he can give himself up to the normal and organic hierarchy of the elements of production, and "represent" his Expression as purely as he desires. In that case—as in the case of a title without an object—the intelligible ideas will be the simple ratification of his desire, but not at all his pretext.

The synthesis of the elements of production cannot be determined by and for itself. If we are familiar with these elements, if we know how to measure their power of expression and their respective limits, if we are able to place them in proper relation—then we possess the means to make their use depend exclusively on the author. That is why the idea of a subject now appears of *technical* importance. The unity of the elements will no longer be regulated in advance and imposed upon the dramatist, as it is by the stage of today; the whole responsibility will be his from the beginning. Consequently, he is obliged to be an artist.

However, although the elements he uses are henceforth at his disposal, yet they are not completely in his hands; to realize his artistic dreams, he doubtless needs collaborators. Will this be a new form of slavery? Barely promoted to the rank of an artist—through the complete possession of his own technique—is he going to fall back again into guardianship, and lose all the advantages of his many sacrifices? What will be the character of such collaboration? Will this collaboration be merely assistance, or will it penetrate deeper—even to the choice of a subject? Let us put aside for the moment the material services that the electrician, the carpenter, and the other artisans will be prepared to offer; they go on by themselves, hierarchically concerned with the body of the actor, which regulates them. Let us consider for the present only those elements which dictate to the life and the movement of that body. Then, afterwards, we shall turn to the body itself, that marvelous intermediary, dominated by the dramatist, but in its turn dominating space.

Our theatrical habits make it very difficult to imagine what freedom in staging could mean, and to visualize a new handling of the elements of production. We cannot conceive of a theatre, it seems, except in terms of the present-day stage—a limited space filled with cut-out paintings, in the midst of which actors pace up and down, separated from us by a clear-cut line of demarcation. Further, the presence of plays and musical scores in our libraries is apparently enough to convince us that a work

· 49

of dramatic art can exist without actual presentation. Reading the play, or playing over the score on the piano, we are convinced that they are living and that we possess them. Otherwise, how can we account for the renown of a Racine or a Wagner? Is it not evident that their work is on these sheets of paper? What does it matter whether we produce their work or not, since these texts, in themselves, can remain immortal? There we are! The dramatic author chooses a form of art that is visual, that is meant for our eyes; yet when he writes it down on paper its fame and glory are assured.

What would Rembrandt amount to, if we had only an account of his pictures? His treatment of color cannot be adequately described, would you say? Why not, if you accept the fallacy that words and sounds can express even warm life in space? If, in a work of dramatic art, this life is only of secondary—indeed, even of negligible—moment, why make so much of it? Why fill our public life with it, and raise costly temples to it? If such is the case, let us consider a dramatic work as a novel in dialogue, or a symphony to be chanted; let us speak no more of it—and let us look at painting or at sculpture. Our body will always be living enough to carry us to our work, our pleasures, our nourishment, and our sleep; for it cannot exist as a book or a musical score, and, besides, it is not immortal.

Look, for example, at *The Theatre of the 19th Century*.[1] Open the book: it analyzes the written play, nothing more. I once knew a little boy who opened with fluttering heart any volume whose title bore the prophetic word *theatre*. He hoped each time to find something more than words there. We are grown up; words are enough.

Our dramatic authors are writers of words. If, in a classic play—that is to say, one whose written words are well known and widely accepted—an actor, through sheer joy in his playing, lets himself go to the extent that he adds or takes away a spoken word, the people cry, "Sacrilege!" What would Shakespeare, the Man of Life, say to that? The true artist is not obstinately

[1 One can only guess what book Appia had in mind.]

attached to a work of art. He bears art in his soul, always living. If one work is destroyed, another will come to replace it. For him, Life is more important than its fixed and immobile representation — and far more important than words! We are so degraded that we place words before life, and hence, in dramatic art, before the very essence of the art; since we are so willing to renounce the integral existence of plays in space, let us hope that their abstract presence on the shelves of our library is thoroughly safeguarded.

And we dare to speak of dramatic art!

Robinson Crusoe, searching his memory for words, used to attempt reconstruction of certain plays he had read in the past. Forgetting himself in his solitude, he began little by little to accompany these words with gestures, with spontaneous pantomime; whenever his memory failed, the gestures became more insistent, taking the place of the words. Soon the joy of this live fiction took possession of the poor solitary creature: he *lived* the play, no longer merely reciting it; and gradually he drew further and further away from the libraries of the continent.

The next day, whether hunting or working, the sight of his hands or of his body filled him with emotion: had this body not held the soul of Othello, for example, and had it not made this soul radiate space? Had his eyes not *seen* Desdemona, and had he not wept over her innocent heart? Words! Ah! he was going to have some, he was going to coin some—words for this body! And thus, through the sight of his own body, a dramatic poet was born in Crusoe. "You want words," he said to himself. "You shall have some, different each time, if necessary. Rich in words, you will fling your wealth royally toward the heavens; for there will always be words—words for you, matchless body! They are your money and your servants. Bid them come; they come. Chase them; they flee. And you, You remain, always rich and complete, overflowing with a life that words do not know! Henceforth you are my library, my symphony, my poem, and my fresco: I possess Art, in you! *I am art!*"

The theatre has become intellectualized. Today the body

is nothing but the bearer and representative of a literary text; its gestures and movements are not *regulated* by the text, but simply *inspired* by it. The actor interprets, according to his own liking, what the author has written; hence his personal importance on the stage is exclusively interpretative rather than technical, with the result that his role is developed according to one conception, while the settings are being painted according to another. Their union is therefore arbitrary and almost accidental. This procedure is repeated for each new play, and the principle remains the same, whatever care we take with the production in other respects.

It is characteristic of theatre reform that all serious effort is instinctively directed toward the *mise en scène*. As for the text of the play, fluctuations in taste result in classicism, romanticism, realism, *etc.*, all of which encroach on each other, combine with each other, approve or disapprove of each other, and make a desperate appeal to the designer-technician without being heard. But in spite of so many varieties of text, we remain in the same place. The detailed scenic indications which the author sometimes adds to the text of his play always have a childish effect, like the little boy who is determined to enter his little countryside of sand and twigs. The presence of the actor overwhelms the artificial construction; the only contact between the two is grotesque, since it accentuates the impotence of the author's effort.

But if one courageously directs his efforts to the *mise en scène* itself, he is surprised to find that he is attacking the *whole dramatic problem*. To be precise: for what existing plays do we wish to reform the stage? What shall be our standard of values? When we consider the stage as something to be stared at, so to speak, as something quite distinct from the audience, it eludes us. What is the stage as a thing apart? Obviously nothing. It is precisely because of this desire to make the stage something in itself that we have strayed so far from Art. At the very start, then, we must clear the table; we must effect in our imagination this apparently difficult conversion, which consists of no longer looking upon our theatres, our stages, our halls, as necessarily existing for spectators. We must completely free the dramatic idea from any such apparently changeless law.

I spoke of halls for spectators. But dramatic art does not exist to present the human being for *others*. The human being is independent of the passive spectator; he is, or ought to be, *living*. And Life is concerned with the living. Our first move, then, will be to place ourselves imaginatively in a boundless space, with no witness but ourselves—just like Crusoe. To set definite proportions in this space, we must walk, then stop, then walk once more, only to stop again. These stopping places will create a sort of rhythm, which will be echoed in us and which will awaken there a need to possess Space. But Space is boundless; the only guide-mark is ourselves. Hence, we are—and should be—its center. Will its measure, then, exist in us? Shall we be creators of Space? For whom? We are alone. Consequently, it will be for ourselves alone that we will create space—that is to say, proportions to be measured by the human body in boundless space.

Soon the hidden rhythm, of which up to now we were unaware, is revealed. From whence does it spring? We know it is there: we even react to it. Under what compulsion? Our inner life grows and develops; it prescribes this gesture rather than another, this deliberate step rather than that uncertain pose. And our eyes are opened at last: they see the step and the gesture that grew out of an inner feeling; they *consider* it. The hand is advanced this far, the foot is placed there: these are the two portions of Space which they have measured. But have they measured these portions consciously and deliberately? No. Then, why just that far and no farther or no nearer? They have been led.

It is not merely mechanically that we possess Space and are its center: it is because we are living. Space is our life; our life creates Space; our body expresses it. To arrive at that supreme conviction, we have had to walk and to gesticulate, to bend and to straighten up, to lie down and to rise again. In order to move from one point to another, we exerted an effort—however small—corresponding to the beatings of our heart. Those heart beats proportioned our gestures. In Space? No! In Time. In order to proportion Space, our body needs Time! The time-duration of our movements, consequently, has determined their extent in space. Our life creates space and time, one through the other. Our living body is the expression of Space during Time, and of Time in Space. Empty and boundless Space—wherein we are placed at the start so that we may effect this essential transformation—no longer exists. We alone exist.

In dramatic art, too, we alone exist. There is no auditorium, no stage, without us and beyond us. There is no spectator, no play, without us, without us alone. We *are* the play and the stage, because it is our living body that creates them. Dramatic art is a spontaneous creation of the body; our body is the dramatic author.

The work of dramatic art is the only one that is truly identified with its author. It is the only art whose existence is certain *without spectators*. Poetry must be read; painting and sculpture, contemplated; architecture, surveyed; music, heard. A work of dramatic art is lived: it is the dramatic author who lives it. A spectator comes to be moved or convinced; therein is the limit of his role.

The work lives for itself — without the spectator. The author expresses it, possesses it, and contemplates it at the same time. A spectator's eyes and ears will never obtain anything but its reflection and its echo. The framework of the stage is but a keyhole through which we overhear bits of life never intended for us.

We have cleared the table, then. Through movement, we have virtually conquered Time with Space. Henceforth, these two are imposed on us neither by the time-units in a text, nor by an arbitrarily prescribed stage; in our hands, they await our orders. Through them, we become conscious of our power, and able to use it in *freely* creating a living work. We have come back to sources; from sources we are going to proceed. No longer will our antecedents be literature and the other fine arts. Now we hold life at its roots, from whence will spring a new sap for a new tree, of which no branch will be arbitrarily grafted. And if, like the other arts, dramatic art is the result of a *modification of relation-*

ships (see the above quotation from Taine), a condition that is unquestionable, it remains for us to find in *ourselves* the modifying factor. If we sought that factor anywhere else, we should have to accept it already fashioned for ends that would be foreign to the life of our body.

In short, we have seen that it is our inner emotional life which gives our movements their time-durations and their essential character. Further, we have learned that music expresses that life for us in a way that is unquestionable, and in a way that profoundly modifies these time-durations and this character. In music we possess an element, *springing from our inner selves,* whose discipline we can accept unconditionally. From music, then, will the work of *living* art be born; the discipline of music will be the principle of culture which will make the new tree fruitful—that is, on condition that we incorporate it into the roots and thus make it organically a part of the whole. The new Being—ourselves—will be placed under the influence of music. To incorporate the art of sound and rhythm into our own organism will be the first step toward *the work of living art;* and, as in all elementary studies, the first step assumes a peremptory importance. On a proper assimilation at this point will depend all further development.

In the preceding chapters we determined the place the body holds in dramatic art, and attempted to draw technical inferences from an organically-founded hierarchy. As long as the Text was our point-of-departure, we oscillated between the timing and the time-span of the words and those of the music. But now we have come to the point where hesitation is no longer possible. We have cleared the table; hence the only thing to do is to begin again at the beginning—that is to say, with the primordial elements. The living presence of the body will create *living* Space and Time, and the incorporation of music into this body will effect that aesthetic *modification* which is the peculiar property of a work of art.

Now, perhaps, the reader understands why this volume is entitled, not "Dramatic Art," but *"Living* Art." To arrive at a clear idea of *living* art (which art is possible without being necessarily "dramatic" in the ordinary sense of the word), it was necessary to go by way of the theatre, since that is all we have. However, the theatre is but one of the forms of *living* art—of the complete art. The present theatrical art makes use of the body for intellectual (if not futile) ends, and inclines to such a degree toward what we have called "indication" that it often tends to be confused with this. Such a confusion is a violence done to the living body—which, unless it is used for pure Expression, is enslaved.

This much is evident, then: we must submit even the Idea of a dramatic art to this appraisal, if we wish to assign it a fixed place in our artistic culture, and if we wish to give it a name. In that case, perhaps, this now illegitimate and unstable art will find sufficient justification; perhaps it will find a firm foundation—which forbidding the trifling tinsel in which the art now appears, will greatly augment its worth and strength. We can already foresee that dramatic art will have to be considered as a special application of *living* art, bearing somewhat the same relation to it that decorative art bears to plastic or pictorial art. And out of this fact will grow the conviction that after all there are but two kinds of art: immobile art and mobile art—fine art (including literature) and *living* art. Music will hold an exceptional position—in the center, as it were, linking the two types of art.

When these principles are understood and accepted, perhaps we shall emerge from anarchy. The art critic, for example, will be able to say as little as this about a painting, and yet be understood: "It is hard to conceive why the artist immobilized his subject in just that way, since the lines of his work suggest no context." Or, concerning a page of a book: "In this description, the reader sees nothing, apprehends nothing; the words seem to move, and the book becomes an incumbrance." Or, apropos of some example of *living* art: "At this point the authors are too plainly trying to suggest an application not artistically justified." Or, again: "These movements are no longer pure Expression, yet the performers are striving to use them without adding 'indication.' The fault lies in an inadequate light-plot, which makes speech seem imperative."

Ignorance of the hierarchy which prescribes how the living body is to be used has involved all our artistic culture in anarchy and irresolution. We seem to have an ever-increasing desire for artistic bodily life; in art, as in every other phase of our existence, movement has become an imperious need. Each of our forms of art tries to express movement at any price (and only the heavens know at what price, often enough!); consequently, each of them encroaches on the other, and very often what we call an artist's "experiments" are merely his efforts to escape the limitations of his own particular art. Only this, we are convinced, can restore things to their respective places: the sight of a living, moving body, which, under the sway of music, has become a work of art.

The writer has heard a renowned dramatist exclaim, after seeing a perfectly executed, but nonetheless simple, exercise in plastic rhythm: "But now I no longer need to write plays!" Returning to his home, he may have continued to write them—but with a new *knowledge,* a knowledge of what he could and could not do, within his own art form. Doubtless other artists, seeing the same performance, would make the same exclamation. The sculptor, returning to his workshop, would probably regard his works and sketches with discomfort. Most of them, he would discover, merely immobilized the marvellous movement he had just followed and contemplated; consequently, most of them were painfully superfluous, in sculpture. Much the same might be true of the architect, whose visions of space and proportion would be subtly modified and clarified. No longer could he think in terms of mere walls and floors . . . From that time on, the living body would haunt him; henceforth, he would have to work for it alone—for the incomparable body.

However, if the sight of the body can in itself exercise such an influence, consider the result of the architect's personal *experience* of artistic movement. He will begin to desire—*for himself,* this time—a certain ordering of space, and to refuse another that formerly he had found beautiful and acceptable. And the sculptor? It will be his terrible, almost painful, function to close up in stone, movement he has experienced in his own flesh. The synthesis demanded of him by the principle of immobility will become increasingly strict; and, if the desire to immobilize one of the seconds of his plastic and *living* happiness ever takes hold of him, it will seem like a bit of irony out of his oblivious past, when he was insensible to the need for synthesis. He will scornfully suppress such a desire—otherwise, he will be proving his incapacity. The degree of influence that *living* Art will exercise on an artist will be the touchstone of his artistic quality.

But there is still more. And this brings us to the Idea of Collaboration, which is inseparable—as we are going to see— from *living* Art, and from its means of realization.

6. COLLABORATION

A N ARTIST who has once sensed the spark of aesthetic movement within his own body will feel the urge to preserve that spark, to embody it in lasting works of art, not merely in fragmentary experiments. Thus he will have to face the problem of *choice* in all its importance. He will fully comprehend that he would lose by trying to transpose subjects suitable only for inanimate art, into *living* Art; it will be clear that the source of inspiration he longs for does not lie in such a process. He will have the same experience each time he tries to realize—to give life to—any subject that could properly serve for any other art. His subject will be *himself*. He had understood this; now he will experience it bodily. What work of art will he alone be capable of developing, without the aid of a literary, plastic, sculptural, or pictorial design?

To simplify our explanation, thus far we have always spoken simply of "the body"; we have even set it solitary in space. Obviously it is the Idea of the living body that we have thus considered as an essential element. It is evident that in approaching the practice of *living* art, one finds himself in the presence of bodies—his own included—and that if the body is the creator of this art, the artist who possesses the Idea of the living body, implicitly possesses all these bodies. The result is that he works, so to speak, with the life that he creates—with the life of living beings without whose collaboration he can create only marionettes. Consequently, the Idea of Collaboration is implicit in the idea of *living* art. *Living* art *implies a Collaboration.*

Living art is social; it is, unconditionally, the social art. Not the fine arts lowered to a plane within the reach of all, but all rising to a plane within the reach of art: this is the ideal. This is merely repeating that *living* art will be the result of a discipline— a discipline which, though it may not affect all human bodies, will at least affect all human souls, through the awakening of bodily feeling. And just as the Idea of the body—the ideal body, if I may use that term—has proved itself aesthetically real, so the Idea of aesthetic bodily feeling will be able to orient and to guide those who still lack the actual experience of plastic movement. For the latter, to be in contact with and to be influenced by persons privileged to know the life of the body, will be precious indeed.

In pedagogy, a rigorous exchange between master and pupil is necessary to a productive discipline. Indeed, what would one be without the other? In *living* Art, conditions will be the same: the forces employed by those executing a study in bodily movements will be automatically transfused into the responsive organisms of the onlookers, thus contributing to ends which the onlookers would find very difficult to achieve by themselves. Through this exchange, the energy spent by either group will— as living power—flow on and on in a constant stream, assuring us, day after day, of the existence of *living* art.

Let us imagine a poet—by which I mean an artist who thinks, who feels, and who sees things sharply and clearly, and who has both the inclination and the ability to express things in words (written or otherwise)—and let us suppose that this poet is possessed of the idea of collaborating in *living* art and in a work representing that art. First of all, he realizes that his choice of subjects can no longer be arbitrary; moreover his introduction to artistic bodily life reveals his whole poetic life more purely, more clearly, more simply. In him the eternal elements of humanity tend to predominate—and to a high degree—over the particulars in which he had formerly found pleasure, and which language by itself can express in surpassing fashion. This language, which was his joy and his naive pride, acquires a new power, for which at first he cannot account. He still has the mastery of it; he feels, indeed, that he has a greater mastery of it than ever before, and that he has learned to endow it with new accents—and yet these accents, as he utters them, seem like a call to other and still newer ones. Keener and clearer and richer of perception, he hears words speak to him in a new language, with new significance and new completeness.

An analyst because he is a poet, he exercises his powers of analysis by facing and questioning the new words. But they do not reply; they remain vibrant with mysterious life, seeming to demand some new gesture on his part, some supreme accomplishment of his great Desire. He holds out his hands, hoping to draw all of them to him, but the words refuse. What should he do? Slowly, solemnly, he finally heeds their *call*. He has understood: the words are calling him. No longer must his hands reach out to grasp: they—together with his entire being—must offer themselves, must *give*. The conversion is accomplished: the collaborator is born in the poet. His choice is made—or, to be more exact, from now on there will be no choice! If he wishes, he will be able to give every movement of his thought to *living* art, rather than locking it up in the symbol of words; for now the expression of his life will be Life. And the words, freed, will resoundingly acclaim their subordination to *living* art, calling upon that art to animate them. The poet has given them up: from *living* art alone does he wish to receive them in return.

Does this mean that the poet will no longer write to be read? Will he cease to be a literary man? Absolutely not! But, like all other artists on intimate terms with *living* art, he will discover that his sense of values is being modified. Things will be put in their places, so to speak, in a way that he had never anticipated. He will realize how many ideas and feelings he had once entrusted to words alone, when they rightly belonged to *living* expression. On the other hand, he will realize how many subjects worthy of his poetic attention he had refused literary expression. The other arts had always attracted him; he had always transposed them, to a minor degree, into his own, experiencing a satisfaction mixed with embarrassment. Such a procedure will be impossible for him now. Whenever the painter, the sculptor, and so on, seem to lean beyond the limits of their respective art forms, *living* art will say to the poet: "Lead them to me." In every sphere of art, *living* art will serve as a regulator, moderator, and liberator; for where there is *living* art, anarchy is impossible. And in this process, the poet plays a very important role, in harmony with the musician.

I have said that music occupies an exceptional position between the immobile arts and *living art,* transposing to life in Time what the immobile arts offer only in Space. The poet shares this position with the musician, though from a different point of view; his role is less peculiarly technical. He suggests the form which the work of art must have to be intelligible; he is the *title,* the scaffolding in the construction of the living building. When the construction is completed, he seems to disappear; but it is he who has supported the weight of the materials during the building process, and has furnished the proportions for the whole. He indicated these proportions even before the building itself actually existed; without him and without his influence there could have been no building. The structure, once it is completed, embodies the spirit of the poet: in the form of the work of living art, he realizes his whole personality. There is not a musical note, not a bodily gesture which does not possess him. He himself must consent to be only the scaffolding for this marvelous work, at first; later, he must yield himself completely.

However, as in all well-handled construction, both the structure of the building and the nature and weight of the materials must be clearly indicated. These indications, wherein the poet will preserve a bit of his personal life, will be the words of the living poem. The musician must yield to these indications. They afford the means to raise the sanctuary; further, they support it and assure its balance. They are the skeleton of the organism into which music breathes life; they are not Expression, but its supports. Collaboration must be broad and spontaneous and mutual. The architect of a work of *living* art, therefore, is both poet and musician, the one conditioning the other — but never existing without the other. Their equilibrium will not depend on equal participation; on the contrary, their respective

62 ·

shares will be variable, conditioned by the laws of equilibrium—that is to say, of the center of gravity. If the musician wishes to sing all by himself, the structure will be in danger; if the poet wishes to speak alone, the structure runs the risk of being mere scaffolding, decorated to a greater or less degree . . . In a fashion, the poet is the container, the musician the bubbling liquid; the poet is the hand that carries and supports, the musician, the precious fashioned materials. Their union — effected, we will remember, through the body—creates a work of *living* art; and this union is so complete that it can express and realize motifs impossible in the immobile arts, and thus free both poet and musician of all that obscured their vision.

When we say poet and musician, we most certainly are not excluding the performers of *living* art! Musical experience, known and felt in our own bodies, can only dispose and direct us toward motifs that *living* art can and must express. At the same time it will lead us to discard—as a result of our more sensitive bodily feelings—motifs destined for immobilization in other arts. *Living* art is a matter of the entire being, and the more its collaborators can bring their whole life to its service, the higher will be is mission. The *living* "craft" is both very simple and very complex. Its theory is simple, since it demands only the complete gift of self; but its application exacts a complex study that few are able to complete. Hence there exists the necessity for Collaboration, or coöperation.

And anyone can see that this principle in itself is a guarantee of the purely human quality of the work; the particulars which, as we have seen, exist in the sphere of mere Indication (in contradistinction to that of Expression) concern individuals more than the group. If, for some reason, such Indication should be temporarily needed, the *living* work would incline toward a dramatic application calling for one author rather than another; the collaborators would have to agree in such cases to be only faithful executors of the wishes of a single one among them, forsaking for a time the more spontaneous collective expression. The life of the work manifests itself in this oscillation between Indication and Expression, which prevents it from crystallizing in a formal aesthetic code. This oscillation sustains attention; it stimulates emotion by the contrasts it sets up; and finally, it permits the individual to shine through more completely than in a prescribed form.

For example, in a great national and patriotic festival, the historical (and to a degree geographical and social) themes have a rather important role to play. They must be present in more than name; they must unfold before us in time and in space. If we present them only in their rational—that is to say, simply dramatic—form, we will render difficult the communication of the eternal values of these themes; at least, those values will not be *represented,* but will remain enclosed within the historic action. In that case—whether we are participants or spectators—we ourselves must silently and consciously deduce these values, the Expression of which will not have assumed artistic form. They will not be revealed as a common blessing, but will remain dependent on the sensibility and the intellect of each separate individual: the human essence of the historic action—*the inner essence of the phenomenon,* to use Schopenhauer's phrase—will have been neither *expressed* nor represented.

It is at this point that the oscillation of which we have spoken will take on its highest social import. The divine emotion must not remain the privilege of some—of those who are able to free it from its accidental coverings; it must be offered in a form clearly accessible to all. The eternal drama hidden beneath historical customs, events, and costumes must be made visible and audible to everyone. And *living* art in its most perfect purity, in its highest idealization, is alone capable of that. The patriotic festival, then, will judiciously oscillate between historically precise dramatic Indication and Expression of its eternally human content without regard to any specific historical epoch. At Geneva, in July 1914, the first act of the June Festival—a grand patriotic spectacle, commemorating the entrance of Geneva into the Swiss Confederation, and composed and staged by Jaques-Dalcroze—presented an imposing and unprecedented example of this aesthetic phenomenon. It realized the *simultaneity* of the two principles. The spectator had simultaneously before his eyes, first, animated historic themes whose progression in itself formed a majestic dramatic action, and, second, their purely human Expression, stripped of all historic pomp, presenting a sacred commentary on—and a transfigured realization of—the events. This two-fold action was a revelation, and was masterfully handled by the author and his collaborators.

We have mentioned the fact that a work of *living* art is the only one that exists completely, without spectators (or listeners). It needs no audience, for it implicitly contains the audience within itself. Since it is a work *lived* throughout a determinate length of time, those who live it—both its creators and its participants — assure its complete existence through their activity alone. If we should come to contemplate such a work, we would add nothing to it. The particular type of personal activity demanded for the contemplation of all other kinds of art is not demanded for this one.

But, on the other hand, *living* art does not sanction the deadly passivity of the audience of our present theatre. What, then, must we do to participate, as it were, in the life of this new work of art? What attitude are we to assume when we are face to face with it? First of all, we must not feel that we are *face to face* with it. *Living* Art is not a representation. We already know that; now we must prove it. How? By turning away, as though the work were unapproachable? No, we cannot do that; from the moment it exists, we are with it, in it. To turn away from a work of *living* art would be to disown our very selves—as, alas, we do on so many occasions in our social life. At least let us not allow this miraculous living thing to flower and to blossom while we passively look on! Let us try the great experience; let us beg the creators of the work to *take us with them*. Then they will seek some connecting link that will engender in us the divine spark. Even though our collaboration *in* the work be small, we shall live with it; we shall discover that we are artists.

It is with profound emotion that the author writes these

last words. In them he locks up all his beliefs; in them he sums up his highest aspirations.

Work is not only the source of contentment, and hence of happiness; it is also the only means of fulfilling any profound desire. Consequently, in whatever sphere we labor, our technique is of capital importance. The great work of an old master in the ancient guilds was, above all, proof of *technical* leadership. These ancient artisans knew how far technique alone could lead them in their striving for beauty. They sought for beauty as a matter of course; probably they never even spoke of it. Technical mastery was the chief object of their discussion and of their effort.

The author, too, is convinced that only the path of *technique* can lead us to a collective universal beauty whose model is the work of *living* art. Under the almost tyrannical sway of this conviction he has drawn up the present volume, and given it form. To wish for the end without acquiring the means is more illusory and more dangerous in art than elsewhere, since art shelters a demon which readily appears as an angel of light—a demon that only scrupulous technical integrity can keep in subjugation. Many attempts at a complete art of universal appeal and influence have miscarried and still miscarry, because of an incomplete technique. We take for the whole work what is only a fragment, and to this fragment we apply processes that are necessarily ineffectual. We have improperly created a sort of classification that considers, for example, all technical attention to objects different from technical attention to individuals. We even name the one practice, the other, theory, forgetting that human theories can become techniques as well, and be transformed into tools for work. Modern sociology, psychology, *et cetera*, have made this discovery, and recognize the value of *the tool*.

In art anarchy still reigns; wishing to place the human body in a hiearchy of usable means—in a set of technical tools —seems Utopian and childish. The artist still considers humanity—his brothers—as a mass which is distinct from himself, and to which he can present his finished work. The aesthetic conversion we have spoken of—which consists, as we have seen, of taking himself as work *and* tool, and then in passing on his feelings and convictions to his brothers—is still unknown to the artist. Even the best intentioned ones still think they are promoting social solidarity and universal art by placing before the poor spectator a work which was never destined for him, and which, moreover, he cannot comprehend in the form it is given.

It is precisely the poor spectator who conditions the technique of living art; without him there is no technique.

And if the author has been obliged to begin at the end rather than the beginning, that is because we still live under an aesthetic misunderstanding which is the inevitable result of a false hierarchy of elements. Had he tried from the outset to present the great Unknown, he would have had to risk being misunderstood. Now, however, strengthened by the knowledge we have gathered, we can retrace our steps in order to gain a view of the whole, for it seems that a misunderstanding is no longer possible.

By this quick backward glance, the author will seek to answer the questions which the reader has doubtless long been asking him: What shall we do to realize our aim? How shall we attack the problem practically; how shall we solve it?

7. THE GREAT UNKNOWN
AND THE EXPERIENCE OF BEAUTY

I N AN AGE when, in every field of knowledge, we are seeking to learn more about ourselves, how can one help being startled by our ignorance concerning our own body, concerning our entire organism, *from an aesthetic point of view?* The magnificent development in sports and general hygiene has given us a taste of movement, fresh air, and sunlight. With good health, physical beauty certainly grows, and physical strength gives man an unmistakable air of freedom which even sometimes borders on an indifference which is a little insolent or inhuman. Once again the body begins to *exist for the eye;* we begin to dress the body, rather than to cover it. Even though many unfortunate and tenacious prejudices still remain—such as viewing an unclothed body with suspicion, or preserving outworn customs of dress simply because we think them prescribed by good education, or by social and professional demands—there is scarcely a middle-class citizen of fifty years ago who would not be greatly surprised at our ease and lack of self-consciousness in this regard. We *feel* our body underneath our clothing, and when we undress, we sense the anomaly in regarding as a precaution of morality (in this sense our morality is always sexual) what is merely a climatic necessity.

The result of all this is that the beauty of the human body is slowly tending to reënter our society. Hypocritically, we still relegate it to our museums and artists' workrooms, with a sigh of embarrassment and tolerance. We are reassured, however: these bodies do not and cannot move. Art immobilizes them, and in this sense at least, they are at rest; public morality and censorship can look upon them. But if they had moved, or if they could move, would they be of marble, or would they be designed and painted? No! they would be beautiful living flesh —and that, it appears, is just what we do not desire.

Do not the discomfort and the curiosity that a wax museum inspires grow out of the fact that the body is represented almost at the point of moving—or even beyond? And that to render that movement plausible it was necessary to imitate this body to the point of deception? On the other hand, do not acrobats immobilized in groups called "plastic" cover their bodies with a uniform color (ordinarily white) to simulate inanimate matter, and hence to make themselves inoffensive "morally . . ."? And when they change their poses before our eyes, in order to reimmobilize themselves differently, is not the instant in which they move puzzling and troubling? Why cover oneself with color if one is moving? Just as immobility in a living body is aesthetic nonsense that no polished coating can justify, so mobility in a polished body is repulsive, since it animates a form which could and should be represented as inanimate. One and both are profoundly immoral, since they pervert our aesthetic taste by misusing what should be most sacred—the human body.

For a great majority, bodily beauty — and hence the naked body—is tolerated only in art, where we accept it inanimate and transfigured. And in spite of what is commonly known as sexual "morality," we tolerate in art the most openly lascivious scenes—some of us because such scenes alleviate the poverty of our public life on this essential point, others because we fear being accused of not understanding the fine arts.

Our modesty grows out of the embarrassment we feel when we expose our body, and out of the fact that we experience the same kind of embarrassment when we see other naked bodies, knowing as we do that these bodies are our own. Unless we repudiate this feeling of discomfort—to put it mildly—we must repudiate *living* art from the beginning, for this art is based on the feeling of the collectivity of human bodies, so to speak, and on the happiness that this collectivity insures. We must, consequently, repudiate all ingenuousness in our general artistic attitude, for art in any form is but the expression of ourselves. The whole history of art bears witness that no compromise is possible. To be an artist is first of all not to be ashamed of one's body—but to love it in all bodies.

If I said that *living* art will teach us that we are artists, I implied that *living* art inspires in us love and respect—not love without respect—for our own body. Such a feeling is a collective one: the artist-creator of *living* art sees in all other bodies his own; he feels in all the movements of other bodies the movements of his own. Thus he lives, *bodily*, in humanity; he is its expression. Humanity is his own — no longer in mere written, spoken, painted, or sculptored symbols, but in the great living symbol of the living body, freely alive.

After good hygiene—and those sports compatible with good hygiene—the aesthetic education of the body is the first step to surmount; its mastery the first rank to achieve. The future of our whole artistic culture—and, obviously the very existence of *living* art—depends on a correct bodily pedagogy. Its importance is incalculable.

And let us not forget — above all, at this point — the serious, almost solemn responsibility that falls on those who achieve even this first rank, since they can never develop too much aesthetic strength in themselves, to pass on a portion to others who, in one way or another, are less privileged. Aesthetic socialism is still unknown. We think we have done well for humanity when we place a work of art within the reach of all, according to the common hypocritical phrase. There are even artists who conceive and execute their work to this end, and who think they are acting wisely. A cake is no nearer the reach of the poor if one puts therein less butter and sugar. The very idea of placing a cake within the reach of the poor is a senseless one. It is *ourselves* that we must place, not within their reach, but where we can give to them.

And when I say "we," I certainly mean, not our works, but our whole person, including the body; and when I say "body,"

I do not mean only our arms to share their labor or support their weakness, but our whole, our entire body. Now, we can do this only by seeing ourselves in their body—and they will feel our gift only if they see themselves in ours. In art we have nothing else to bring them. This gesture is the point-of-departure; thereon depends all of *living* art. We dare not offer the less fortunate ones fruits swelled with a strength which is not theirs, ripened under a sun which is not theirs—fruits which they could never assimilate. We need no longer draw them to us; nor need they draw us to them. We must mutually recognize ourselves in each other. The ray of light that will foster this divine penetration must find an atmosphere where it can be diffused in a constant splendor. From an aesthetic point of view, this atmosphere is our body—possessed in common by everyone, for a definite artistic end.

The inhabitants of Tahiti could conceive of love or friendship only if the two people concerned had been afraid *together*. Their life was so calm that a very forceful impression —growing out of a *common experience*—was necessary for the union of their souls. In our life—leveled and monotonous to the point where the worst disorders, the cruelest sufferings are insufficient to disturb our social torpor, to light up our accumulated egotism and our barbarous dilettantism—the ineffable joy of art *experienced in common with others* can sanctify our fraternal union. To feel in common with others does not signify merely having the same pleasure with others (as in a concert hall, or at a spectacle), but being animated throughout one's whole being —body as much as soul—with the same *living* and active flame. It means "being afraid together" in the all-powerful embrace of beauty; it means having accepted together the creative impulse and its responsibilities.

Robinson Crusoe, in his cruel solitude, had to create beings to rejoice and suffer with him, to use a phrase of Prometheus. He had to see these beings in his own body, and the reciprocal gift we have mentioned above was impossible for him except in a dramatic fiction, except in a special application of *living* art. Since dramatic art exists to express emotions not necessarily present in our personal life at the moment—hence, fictitious emotions—he was readily able to "be afraid" with the persons of his creation. But he was alone: even the gift he made for himself was fictitious—although his work, of course, was real and living!

Perhaps we are all as solitary as Robinson Crusoe, but —praised be you, O Prometheus—we are that in common with others like ourselves! Let us be thankful that when we recognize ourselves in our brothers, it is in another body than ours, another real body. And let us remember, too, that for us who are not alone, dramatic fiction is not the only opportunity for union with others, as it was for Robinson Crusoe; the aesthetic modifications that music prescribes are sufficient to unite our souls by uniting our bodies. The Great Unknown, our body—*our common body,* so to speak—is within that music; we can sense its silent presence, like a latent, expectant force. At times we even feel a bit of the joy that is waiting there . . . Let loose that joy; art can give it to us!

Let us learn to live art in common with others; let us learn to free ourselves, to experience in common the deep emotions that bind us together. Let us be artists! *We can.*

It is our habit to consider the artist's existence as more independent than ours; we pardon him more readily than we pardon others, mixing our admiration with envy. Our admiration is inspired by the disinterested character of his art, which we trace back to him, so that we may find an excuse for his several weaknesses. Then, after we have accorded him the right to live more or less in freedom and in a very advantageous light, we proceed to envy him. We all perceive that such a mode of life develops in him faculties we do not possess—faculties that seem to earn for him happiness and influence. We do not observe, however, that any activity with whose details we are unfamiliar and from whose results alone we must judge, inspires this same type of admiration and envy. The person of a great philosopher, astronomer, chemist, and so on, is separated from ours by the mysteries of his work.

An uncommon activity, then, must evidently exert a very particular influence on the character; we think so, at least, and are inclined to account for all originality and distinctiveness in terms of this influence. An unfamiliar activity thus inspires us with admiration; but at the same time it separates us from the individual who is engaged in it. We are as clearly separated from the philosopher as we are from the artist; socially, we maintain the status of a spectator in relation to both. We are always holding out a hand toward such men—to take what we can. We would not think of asking a business man for money, because we feel ourselves equal to him; yet we beg all our lives from those whose activity seems distinct enough from ours to permit it.

It is quite clear that we are always expecting something from the artist, with no regard for what we could offer him in return. If we use money as an intermediary, we remain the artist's debtor. We know that a pair of shoes is made with money, so after we have paid our shoemaker, we think of other things. But when we contemplate a work of art which we have bought, we feel that we have given nothing in return which can be compared with it—and that this work of art, after all, is not for us. "Property of Mr. X" is a misleading label. When a man buys a patent, he knows well enough that he is not buying the invention. Nothing can be offered in exchange for a great discovery; nothing in exchange for a work of art. Both of them remain forever the property of the artist and the genius. The use of money as an intermediary merely accentuates the fact that we are but spectators.

When we buy a ticket for a concert, a play, or a lecture, our unfortunate relationship to the presentation is manifest. To stand in line at a box office is humiliating; most of us, under such circumstances, try not to notice . . . However, our life is a perpetual line before the ticket window of the artist, of the scholar, of the man of renown. We persist in believing that things are bought, but if we open our purse to buy them, with money or without, we only deliberately close and lock the door of our individuality. The only thing we can give in exchange is ourselves; we know this and we refuse: the same contemptible shame that forbids us to show our body prevents us, likewise, from uncovering our soul. And we complain of isolation!

An unprejudiced person who has, in the right spirit, ever observed earnest and determined Christians—they are rare—and has followed them for some time, observing their acts, their words, their looks, and their gestures, has had to exclaim, "These are artists!" As a matter of fact, these exceptional people, hour after hour, fulfill the only essential requirement for a work of art: the gift of self. And their life would be a work of art if we knew how to possess it—that is to say, to give ours in exchange. In this sense, we have several works of art; we possess not one.

Ah yes! We are isolated by the bolts of our jail; we receive our pittance only through a tiny window. How should we know then, what goes on outside that window? There lies the mystery that impels our respect and admiration; there lies the liberty that fills us with envy! The artist? It is he who lives outside the little window that marks our limitations and our pitiable dependence.

Such conditions have inevitably created abnormal forms of art. A life in prison is not a normal life. Modern art is art that is destined for prisoners. And an artist can no more give himself to prisoners than prisoners can give themselves to him; a bolted door separates them.

Henceforth we must look to the present forms of art for neither precept nor example. Our only desire is to escape from prison, to breathe pure air—and to breathe it in common with everyone. All work inspired during our captivity we shall leave behind us, in the sad corridors wherein we vegetated. And our hands, freed, will no longer be held out to receive, but to give. What does it matter that they are empty: other hands will come to grasp them, to fill them with their own living warmth, and to receive it back again in return.

And thus the immortal pact will be consummated. All of us will wish to *live* art, not merely to enjoy it! Again face to face with each other, we will no longer oppose each other as we used to do in our theatres and libraries; we will penetrate each other. Pale reflections from outside will no longer light up our eyes . . . No! our eyes will cast their own flame into space, creating *living* light across *living* space, in the transfiguration of time. And what does it matter if our first steps are awkward; we *will be living art*: or better, through art we will be learning to *live*. We will be able to smile in commiseration at the sight or the sound of works of art whose artificial perfection was the only fruit of our former slavery.

Our touchstone from now on will be the experience of beauty—experience in common with others. All of us will be *responsible* for our own works; we no longer need concern ourselves with the materials or the motives for those done by others. Our works will be the supreme result of our whole life, expressed through a body—our body—and subject to the austere discipline of beauty. Our aim lies in this life-activity itself; as soon as it is attained, we pass beyond it. Life exists in Time: as soon as it is realized, the past swallows it up, the future claims it, and time accords it no leisure for idleness . . . Especially in this sense must art be lived!

We are going to leave behind us art dealers and book-collectors, with their cobwebs. A book, a musical score, a picture, a statue, will have only a relative value: to afford education or information, to inspire emotion or recall memories, to preserve a cultural attainment. Schopenhauer assures us that every great man, in every sphere of human activity has always said—or wished to say—precisely "the same thing." We feel this "thing" beat within us, always more insistent, always more inspiring. Freed from the chains of Form, we are going to shout out this "thing," each in his own way—as certain of its supreme reality as we are of the victory over our whole being.

By giving us the key to our personality, the Experience of Beauty will make us conscious of the limitations of our daily life, and will teach us patience and serenity. For amid the dreary or depressing circumstances of life, it will keep alive a glowing hope, like that of the artist when he beholds the destruction of a beautiful work of art—perhaps even his own, as in the case of Leonardo da Vinci—and yet feels within himself the power to create a thousand new ones . . .

But the new power will not be merely a joy; the development of a new power implies the development of a new responsibility. The gift of self will carry with it new obligations. The gift in itself is not enough; we must look to the value and the quality of what we have to offer.

Since the experience of beauty has resulted from a *new* consciousness of our body, the idea of this body now takes on an import that we had not suspected—or that we had forgotten.

So far the author, concerned as he was with the technical necessities of his subject, has had to name the *body* by that term alone. More than one reader, perhaps, has been offended by my insistence in this regard, or has been surprised that I failed to temper its use by a single qualification. As a matter of morality, we are accustomed to give this word the meaning of merely an organism—an organism subject to such dangers for the spirit that we have had to draw a sharp line of demarcation between them. It is useless to recall what degrees of hypocrisy and ugliness this criminal principle has forced us to. On the other hand, it is becoming necessary to remember that in this book we mean by "body"—the human body—the visible form of our whole being, and that this word possesses one of the richest connotations our life can grant. Hence, though the author has often had to use it to designate simply a mobile form in space, he has never lost sight of its supreme connotations.

The moment to affirm those connotations has come; we have arrived at the point in our study where the responsibility for our whole being—including the merely physical body—enters vitally into the reckoning.

Even as long as it was merely a question of time or of space, of two or of three dimensions, of movements or of time-durations—even then the worth of the term "body" should have been readily understandable; it should have been evident that we would not pay such careful aesthetic attention to an organism without a soul, to a simple machine! But now any possible misunderstanding must be cleared up. We have seen that the artistic value of the moving body constitutes an important technical problem to solve for the future of our culture. When the author has convinced the reader of the obligations which this value imposes on our whole being and on its relation to public life, he will be ready to bring the present study to a close. Each one, then, can estimate for himself the place he occupies—or should occupy—within the limits of his age and social position, of his degree of culture and personal ability, in order to be a *living* artist, a representative of the *life* of art.

This life rewards its disciples with a radiance that no negative influence can dull. It is a positive, burning flame within us. A real and personal Presence within us can of itself—directly and without any intermediary—project this divine light, with or without words, with or without works of fixed form and limits. The slightest gesture reveals it.

By developing ourselves as much as possible, then, by taking active or sympathetic parts in every manifestation of public life, by giving ourselves without reserve and without compensation, but also without compromise, we can prepare for the joyous future of *living* art.

In another treatise the author is planning to return to the subject of the social influence of a *life* of art, and to enlarge upon its consequences.[1] He is already beginning to notice precursory symptoms. For example: public halls of all types are no longer used for one—and only one— purpose. Political and religious gatherings, concerts, conferences, and so on, are frequently given in a circus hall or in a theatre; on the other hand, theatres are freely made over into circus halls. Specific labels

---

[1 These plans were partly carried out in *Art Vivant ou Nature Morte?* (Milan: Bottega di Poesia, 1923), first published in *Wendigen* 9 and 10 (Double Number, 1921). An English translation by S. A. Rhodes was published in *Theatre Annual*, Vol. II (1943).]

that have been rigorously fixed on the façades of public buildings for years are beginning to be blown to the four winds. Music and the dance have entered the *Comédie Française* and drama *L'Opéra*. Our private and public lives are no longer strictly fixed and limited. The family hearthstone extends beyond the narrowing walls of our homes, and the life of the outside world bursts in at our windows; the telephone makes our conversations almost public. We are even beginning to lose our fear of exposing our bodies—and, therefore, our souls.

Thus, we are beginning to feel an ever more imperious need to unite with others. But where shall we unite? In the open air, or else in a hall not limited to this or that particular use— a hall whose sole reason-for-being is to permit us to unite with each other, as in the cathedral of the past . . .

The term escapes me: I cannot recall it. Yes: it is in a *cathedral of the future* that we need to take our new vows! Let us refuse henceforth to dash from one place to another for activities which we must watch as spectators, and whose form we cannot penetrate. Let us seek a place where our newly-born community of purpose can be clearly asserted—a place flexible enough to afford the realization of our every desire for a complete Life.

Perhaps then other labels will fly away in their turn like dead leaves: perhaps "concert," "presentation," "conference," "exhibition," "sport," and so on, and so on, will be abandoned as names forever. Overlapping in purpose and function, perhaps they will merge into one. And each of us, then, perhaps, can *live* his life in common with everyone else, instead of watching it trickle away in diverse channels, between impervious walls.

8. BEARERS OF THE FLAME

Parmi la foule sans lumière
qui suit le chemin gris des jours,
quelqu'un surgit soudain, frémissant, ébloui,
heureux! . . . Heureux!
Sûr d'un triomphe intérieur,
il bondit, brandissant sa joie
comme une torche!
Son ivresse palpite et brûle dans sa main
comme une flamme
qui le vent froisse
et déroule!
Et la lumière qu'il brandit
éclaire les visages proches
de la foule . . .
Elle se propage et grandit.
Et, plus leur ivresse rayonne
et gagne, et grise d'autres coeurs,
plus ces porteurs ardents d'invisibles flambeaux
ont des visages sûrs et beaux
que baigne le vent de leur course!
Puisque prodiguer son bonheur,
c'est en être plus riche encore.

Jacques Chenevière

HAVING EXTENDED my investigations to the farthest limits of the problem in hand, I fear that I may have over-reached my rights as far as the reader is concerned. Yet such a procedure seemed indispensable to me; for if one intends to grasp an object firmly in his hand, he must first overreach that object. It is the same with an idea. Now that we have taken possession of *living* art, of the Idea it represents, and of the responsibilities it imposes, let us seek a clue to the practical usage it requires if it is to be of any benefit to our modern culture.

So far it has been only by accomplishing sacrifice after

· 79

sacrifice that we have been able to arrive at the essence of what Movement—that is to say, *Life*—represents in art.

We have had to proceed negatively on almost every point, in order to grasp each successive idea as firmly and as solidly as possible. Now we are on intimate terms with both ourselves and others like us—with no intermediary except a mutual desire for aesthetic communion. Specifically and practically speaking, how are we going to express this desire; how are we going to share it with others, concretely and convincingly, so as to inspire them to unite with us in realizing the Great Work?

A purely restrictive attitude—a passive but insistent renunciation of everything in modern life that contradicts *living* art—would probably merely discourage and depress those whose confidence we hoped to gain. If we assumed such an attitude, would we not be mistaking the letter for the spirit? In that case, who would lead the way? Who would orient us, if those who hold the key lock up its secrets in a hidden chest, on the pretext of avoiding compromise?

Living art, as we have seen, demands a new *attitude* on the part of the dramatic author—and this attitude, in turn, demands that he concentrate his imagination on the living body alone. In a sense, all of us have now become dramatic authors, and all of us must change our attitude. In his work, a dramatic author must accept elements of humanity of which he disapproves; out of that very conflict his work draws life. *Our* dramatic work is our public and private life; and if we repudiate its destructive elements, we repudiate then and there our dramatic work—our work of *living* art. Our reaction in this regard clearly indicates our attitude. At one now with *living* elements from the beginning, we must—like the dramatist—dominate the conflicts and reactions to a greater end. We who know living art and its possibilities bear a torch of life, which must light up the innermost recesses of our public and especially our artistic life. We cannot guide others by placing our torch in a private sanctuary, before idols that only we love and worship. I have said that

80 ·

every profoundly sincere Christian is an artist: he is that because he gives himself, never refusing contact with those he wishes to know and perhaps assist.

Like such a Christian, let us be dedicated followers. Like him, let us jealously guard the source that nourishes our torch—but let us bear its flame above our heads as a grand token. Wherever we are, let us use it to light up the surrounding space for those who share that space with us; it will awaken unknown splendors, it will cast revealing shadows. Thus we will prepare— by striving together, surely like brothers—the new space that our new vows require, *living* Space for our *living* beings.

In our search for the flame of aesthetic truth, we had to extinguish, one after the other, the false torches of a false artistic culture. Now our own fire—yours and mine—can relight those torches.

Let us not abandon them to a pitiable, smouldering existence. Our only right henceforth is to light up, not to abandon. If we wish to be happy together, we must first of all suffer together: this is the essential principle of art, and the strongest reason for *living* art.

In our day, *living* art is a personal *attitude* which should be shared in common by all men. To insure this, we who possess it must cherish and preserve it wherever life brings us together. To give it up is the only compromise, the only interdiction.

DESIGNS

These few sketches are not, properly speaking, illustrations of the preceding pages. The reform of the *mise en scène* must be accompanied by a new conception of dramatic art: an art so closely related to our personal and our social life that it is impossible to discuss it without upsetting many conceptions and habits which seemed almost immutable, or at least, too deeply rooted to be changed all at once. A drama on the stage, from whatever angle one looks at it, is a reproduction of a fragment of our life. By this I do not mean that it is a mirror of our manners, as we have been wont to say it is. Our inner life, its joys, its pains, and its conflicts, is entirely independent of our manners, *even when these manners seem to be determining factors*. The human passions are eternal—eternally the same; manners merely color them superficially, just as the form of a costume indicates an epoch. But the soul hidden beneath the costume is timeless; it is simply the human soul. From the dramatic point of view, a fragment of our existence is a fragment of the story of that soul. Consequently, the form we give to our productions either fits this definition and need not be changed; or, on the contrary, it is based on inertia or conservatism, and therefore is anachronistic. The question has two sides: one artistic, the other purely human and social, since the theatre is a joy we share with others. Here I must be permitted to make some remarks which, while explaining these sketches, will also clarify the work which has preceded them.

The artistic side of the question is concerned with the technical means we use in the theatre, and with our manner of employing them. Thus we can readily see that in dramatic art technique is dependent on our conception of the art itself. Theoretically, this conception should be open to discussion, for inquiry is still permissible—if only the force of inertia did not hold the dramatist to a form that is rigid and unable to follow the evolution of our thought and taste. Practically, however, it is first necessary to adapt our technique to the plays now in existence; this is very inconvenient, since there is interdependence between the dramatic form and the production form. Nevertheless, it seems obvious that the former should take the lead, for one would hardly wish to create a new technique for works as yet non-existent. The balance, it is true, is not constant. The dramatist can, on occasion, go beyond the technical methods offered to him; and, on the other hand, technical methods can momentarily pass him by, in such a way that new technical methods will bring with them a new development in the dramatic form.

Hence, if a dramatic work cannot find a suitable production form in the contemporary theatre, it is because, on the one hand, the dramatist did not pay attention to the means at his disposal; on the other, because the *mise en scène* did not keep up with evolution of taste demonstrated in the work.

In the year 1876, Richard Wagner inaugurated his theatre at Bayreuth. He felt such a move necessary, since nowhere else could he find the exceptional atmosphere and other factors essential for an art work which deliberately broke with the conventions and traditions of his epoch.

Of what did his reform consist? Was it essentially technical? Assuredly not. Wagner, taught by a long and painful experience, had perceived that dramatic art is an exceptional art, and that its exceptional character must be recognized, lest it decline and die. His life was tending more and more toward a dramatic *coup d'état*; his productions were gradually taking on the decisive characteristics of this *coup d'état*; and it was only at the price of innumerable compromises and extraordinary personal suffering that he succeeded in producing his dramas on the contemporary stage. At Bayreuth he was at least free! There he could give his productions their exceptional character, and thereby endow them with a new power. Much has already been said about this subject. The arrangement of the auditorium and the placement of the orchestra are equally well known.

The prodigious musical evolution—which we insist on crediting to Wagner the *musician,* though Wagner the *dramatist* should carry the responsibility—has been, for a long time, part of our modern technical knowledge. His influence, unfortunate from a musical standpoint, has been recognized but the harm has been done. Obviously we cannot alter the aim of what is a technical debt—*as we have done*—with impunity.

Without his music, Wagner ran the risk of failing to attract our attention; with it, he has spoiled us, for we have taken the musical form for the dramatic spirit.

Wagner did not wish to compose his music as he did, but he was compelled to do so by his new dramatic conception, which he was impelled above all else to reveal to us. Upon analysis, we find that he was essentially a dramatist. If, in spite of Bayreuth, he has not succeeded, that is because his work contains within itself a profound contradiction. The author of this volume has been particularly sensitive to the dilemma in Wagner and his work; the suffering the author has experienced has guided him on the road to a freedom for which the work of the great master is only a point-of-departure, or, if you prefer, an imposing and salutary warning.

Richard Wagner made but one essential reform. Through the medium of music he conceived a dramatic action whose center of gravity lay inside the characters, and which at the same time could be completely *expressed* for the hearer—expressed no longer only by words and gestures, but by a positive development which could fully exploit the emotional content of that action. He wished, moreover, to place this dramatic action on the stage, to offer it to our eyes; but there he failed! Gifted in dramatic technique—like no one before him—with a power that was almost incommensurable, Wagner believed that the *mise en scène* would result automatically. He did not conceive of a staging technique different from that of his contemporaries. A greater care and still greater splendor in the settings seemed to him sufficient. Without a doubt the actors, insofar as they were entrusted with the new action, were the object of his special attention; but—and this is a truly strange fact—although he fixed their action minutely, and thus refined the deplorable contemporary operatic conventions, he then found it natural to place around and behind them painted wings and drops, whose nonsense reduced to nothing every effort toward harmony and aesthetic truth in his *productions* of drama. Was he conscious of his failing? That would be difficult to say positively, though in a pamphlet concerning the presentation of *Parsifal* at Bayreuth in 1882 (several months before his death), he wrote that he felt the *representation* of his dramatic art was still in its infancy.

In summary: the Wagnerian reform concerns the very conception of drama; Wagner's music is the result of it; and the whole gives his works a level so high that they must be looked upon as sacred and unique. In fact, Wagner looked upon all dramatic art as sacred and unique; therein he is a Forerunner. But he did not know how to make his production form—his *mise en scène*—agree with his adopted dramatic form. Thus, so different were his intentions from their visual realization that all his work was weak and disfigured—to the degree that only a small majority could comprehend what it was all about. Such is still the case; and one can assert, without exaggeration, that no one has yet *seen* a Wagnerian drama on the stage.

Simple though the subject appears, it is almost inextricably complicated. Moreover, Wagner's situation is immortally tragic. It will be difficult for one who comprehends and wishes to save what remains of the master's admirable work, to labor with complete composure: the face of the Giant of Bayreuth always looms before him. Notwithstanding, he can pay respect to Wagner only if he himself remains perfectly free; and this liberty can be acquired *only* by a thorough and minute knowledge, line by line, measure by measure, of the master's works.

Such has been the attitude of the writer in searching and *in finding in these very scores* the scenic decorations that some of these designs represent. He has attempted to weaken, as far as possible, the Wagnerian contradiction; to take the *living* actor as the point-of-departure; and to place that actor not before, but in the midst of, planes and lines which are rightly intended for him, and which harmonize with the spaces and the time-units dictated by the music of his role. Since in Wagner music was the source of dramatic inspiration, the writer has sought in the music of these dramas the visual evocation compatible and consistent with that inspiration. Doubtless he has attained only a compromise so far; but that compromise is a conscious and deliberate one, and can pretend to come as near as possible to an integral harmony that Wagner barely dreamed of, though his work bears promise of it.

These remarks have attempted to clarify the reader's understanding of the designs which apply to Wagner's dramas; they naturally demand of the reader at least an approximate knowledge of the plays in question. The designs which then follow (*i.e.*, the "Rhythmic Spaces")—as the reader will notice —are a development of the same principles, though they lack the positive basis of a specific drama. They are, then, simple suggestions to the end of establishing a style under the control of the human body—which is itself stylized by music. Gradually stripped of the romanticism inherent in Wagner's work—romanticism which, of course, one is obligated to retain there—they attain a sort of classicism from which everything that does not stem from the living and mobile presence of the actor is eliminated. They are Spaces intended for the body's sovereign presence. Their particular development and their dimensions remain to be fixed by individual works for which they are used.

Anyone can see, from these general considerations, the path that the writer has followed, almost in spite of himself. Starting out with the depressing feeling that made him sense the Wagnerian contradiction and the irreparable misconception it established, he has finally founded on that very contradiction a scenic principle which is no longer arbitrary or conventional, but which is *organically* constructed on a correct hierarchy of the production elements—a procedure which takes the living and plastic form of the actor as a starting point. In his book, *Music and Theatrical Production* (published in German in 1899 at Munich, by Hugo Bruckmann),[1] he developed this principle and its dramatic and technical results in fairly great detail.

In that era, Wagner's work was all that could serve as a point-of-departure; hence, that book was still under the influence of Wagner, surpassing, however, the necessarily limited range of Wagner's work. Since that time, the writer has had several conclusive experiences in staging: at Paris, Dresden, and Geneva, and especially at the Institut Jaques-Dalcroze. In addition to the present volume, the author has written several articles and pamphlets, and has published designs in the periodicals of several countries. Slidies, and so on, have been made from his designs . . . Jaques-Dalcroze, through his happy creation of Eurhythmics, has definitely confirmed what the writer had foreseen; for, as early as 1895, long before the beginnings of Eurhythmics, the author had written, in *Music and Theatrical Production,* that it was absolutely necessary to find a type of "musical gymnastics" in order to train the actor in musical time and proportion. The present volume gives the technical story of the evolution of the author's theories, and follows them to their conclusions. These designs do not go quite that far! But the kind reader will perhaps find them sufficiently attractive to lead him into the marvelous future of the *living* art to which he has just been introduced. And if he will place himself imaginatively in the midst of these spaces, he will be able to evoke a drama of which he will be an integral part, and a drama which ought to be, for us all, an ideal to pursue unceasingly, no matter what forms it may take.

Ad. Appia.

---

[1]Written in French under the title *La Musique et la Mise en Scène,* the work has been published only in this German translation by Princess Elsa Cantacuzène entitled *Die Musik und die Inscenierung.*]

ADOLPHE APPIA

DESIGNS FOR WAGNERIAN DRAMAS

These designs, chosen from those of the author's romantic period, go back about twenty-five years. They are based on scenarios derived from the scores and worked out minutely, measure by measure. When a design springs from a poetic-musical work, it is so intimately tied to the score that it cannot be understood without such a scenario—which is a transposition of the score in terms of space. It is impossible here to give even an approximate idea of the work involved, and the author must be content with minimum orientation.

PARSIFAL, ACT I: THE SACRED FOREST

In the music, this forest represents a *Temple*. It must have that character—all the more so because the Temple of the Holy Grail itself gradually takes its place at the end of the act. Accordingly, the lines and the general arrangement of the trees will fit in with this architectural arrangement.

Then, when this forest-temple is slowly and solemnly withdrawn from our view, to lead us as in a dream to the divine Temple, during the unreal and tragic splendor of the music, the trunks will little by little lose their roots and be based on flat stones; the vegetation will disappear; the natural light of day will give way to the supernatural light of the supernatural Temple, and the stone columns will gradually and smoothly replace the great shafts of the forest: thus we will pass from one Temple to another.

Parsifal, ACT I

PARSIFAL, Act II: the Keep of Klingsor's Castle

Klingsor, the evil magician, has built his castle on the emptiness and blackness of lost hopes. In the dreadful dungeon of moral despair, he conjures up the means of Parsifal's destruction. In the middle of a grim scene, the young hero appears on the luminous plain. We do not see him, but Klingsor—standing down right on the terrace overhanging the abyss—has seen him in his magic mirror.

Parsifal, unaware of the danger that threatens him, and quite alone, lays siege to the castle. Klingsor, the better to watch and call out in mixed ecstasy and scorn, then quickly climbs toward the luminous sky and leans against the tower which dominates the horizon. In order to emphasize the contrast, the open air will be a most intense blue, while in the depths below the leaden horror of suffering and death will prevail.

Soon afterwards, the entire setting gives way to a garden, perfumed with living and full-voiced flower maidens.

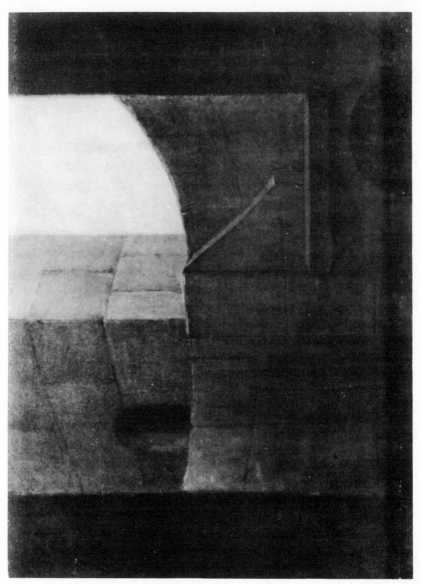

Parsifal, Act II

PARSIFAL, Act III: the Flowery Meadows

We are again on the holy ground of the Grail. The tree trunks and the general appearance of the countryside make this clear. Utter calm is doubtless indicated; but the lines of the mountain imply a striving toward a final resolution.

Indeed, Parsifal is still seeking Amfortas, to heal him and bring peace to him; but after long years of wandering, he no longer hopes to find the secret road to the Temple again, the road of pure and simple hearts. He appears upstage center, coming from the plain. At first we see only the upper part of his body, for the climb is difficult; then, finally, we see all of him, in his black armor. At the threshold of the hut, Gurnemanz, silent with astonishment, watches him pass by. The sacred spring bubbles out from the middle of the rocks. There Parsifal will find rest and assurance for his divine mission. To the left is the thicket which, at the beginning of the act, shelters the sleeping Kundry.

In the clear light of Good Friday, distant bells announce the funeral ceremonies for Titurel. The three figures then climb toward the right, among the tree trunks; the forest soon surrounds them, then moves almost imperceptibly from stage right to stage left—and we are again in the temple of the Grail.

Parsifal, Act III

TRISTAN, Act III

"An abandoned castle in Brittany," Richard Wagner tells us. However, nothing in his text expresses what he implies in that simple statement. Two words of Kurwenal, at the beginning, are enough to orient us. Then we are placed, by the author himself, between the light of day, which blinds and tortures a sick man, and the beneficent dark in which that sick man finds rest by losing consciousness. *That is all.* For assuredly it is not with the eyes of Kurwenal that we must live this hour of passion, without precedent in any literature. Daylight increases Tristan's delirium; Isolde lives in this light, and Tristan is not by her side. Darkness, on the contrary, unites their two souls. Suddenly a great certainty has broken through the heart of this darkness, like a divine ray: Isolde draws near, the wind swells the sails of her ship—Tristan *sees* her in a vision. Then reality proves compassionate: the sail appears on the horizon. Blessed be the light! Joyous, the blood that spurts from the wound and shines brightly in the setting sun! Oh, happy, this last ray of the sun, for it brings Isolde! But alas, to meet this light, and to be lost in it, the torch of night must be put out.

If we except certain indications necessary to place the action, the setting for this act has a single objective: to surround a sick man like a screen, by which Kurwenal tenderly protects his master and his friend. In this abstract setting, the all-powerful lighting will emphasize the significance of light itself, which is of special dramatic value in this act: as long as the light of day torments Tristan, it will not touch him; but, from the moment when the light is identified for him with Isolde's arrival, it will little by little spread until it illuminates his head. Then, the light of dusk will fall, reverently, on the two united lovers.

This entire setting is "practicable." Actually, the author would simplify it even further, and would omit the branches of the trees. The left-hand corner is a kind of geological edging for the setting, somber and neutral in color, which allows the actor to play in the downstage plane of the setting without necessarily being on the horizontal plateau of the main portion of the stage. The author often uses this device.

Tristan, ACT III   OPENING

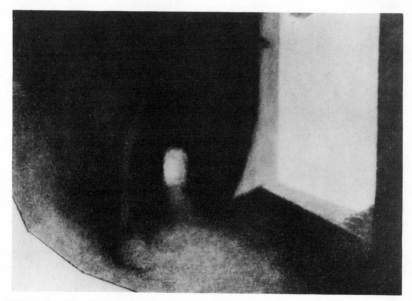

Tristan, ACT III   CLOSE

THE RHINEGOLD: Valhalla

By order of Wotan, the credulous giants have built in a single night the fortress which is to protect the gods and justify their perjury. Hence, Valhalla is a structure of guilt, built upon stratagems and put together by coarse maneuverings. The Rhine separates it from a turf-covered summit which in Wagner is not unlike a drawing-room where the gods prattle away their time and settle—not without elegance—less than commendable quarrels. However, just as in many drawing-rooms, two doors stand menacingly: one, on the right, leads to the gloomy forges of Alberich; the other, on the left, will ultimately serve as an entrance for Erda—she whose ideas dominate the vain knowledge of the gods.

This setting is essentially an open-air setting, and light plays a decisive role in it. The entire summit is "practicable." On the rock to the left Froh is placed; on that to the right, which looks down on the river, Donner, the god of thunder, calls for the storm, and then traces out, above the valley, the illusory rainbow for the entrance of the gods to their fraudulently acquired home.

The Rhinegold

VALHALLA

THE ROCK OF THE VALKYRIE

On this rock Wotan renders powerless the only woman who knows his most secret wish. For Brunhild has not agreed to the cowardly compromises demanded by her father. This setting returns four times in the *Ring of the Nibelungs,* and thus leads the spectator, always afresh, back to the most sensitive point in the drama. Hence it has the importance of a character and must be treated as such. But Wagner demands the impossible. He wishes a summit on which a second summit is mounted; an immense fir tree must shade Brunhild's sleep, and a cave must welcome her with Siegfried. A cave at the pinnacle of a mountain is a rare thing, indeed; and the mass of a large fir ruins the effect of a summit.

Nonetheless, the author has sought to reconcile the irreconcilable; and the score of the four scenes (*The Valkyrie, Siegfried,* and two in *The Twilight of the Gods*) has guided his drawing-pencil.

The study of this setting has revealed to him the role of the ground plan in a Wagnerian drama. Here is a summary of this point: the more the dramatic expression turns inward and for that reason loses contact with outward appearances, the more the actor must tend to use the downstage area—as a consequence removing himself from the background of the setting. On the contrary, the more the poetic-musical expression turns outward and develops the importance of the environmental qualities in the setting, the more the actor must tend to play upstage within the setting. As an example, for Act II of *The Valkyrie*: the intimate duet of Brunhild and Wotan is wholly inward in expressiveness; hence, the downstage area. But when Wotan puts Brunhild to sleep, he takes over the middle area, up to the point where the setting itself (the inclined rock on the right) accepts the sleeping Valkyrie and blends her completely into the countryside. In *Siegfried,* Act III, the nuances in the use of areas are infinite; so also in the Waltraute scene in Act I of *Twilight of the Gods.*

THE ROCK OF THE VALKYRIE

The Valkyrie, ACT III   OPENING

The Valkyrie, ACT III   WOTAN APPROACHES

The Valkyrie, ACT III

PROMETHEUS

These two designs are from a middle period, between the period when I accepted Wagnerian romanticism and my later freedom from it. They were done for a scenario intended for the *Institut Jaques-Dalcroze* and are dated 1910.

The first represents the workshop where Prometheus creates men in his own image. Betrayed by Pandora, Prometheus transfers his creatures to a happy isle. That is the second act, for which there is no design here. But he is soon rejoined by his enemies, who chain him to the pediment of his ruined workshop. Finally, delivered from his chains by Hercules, Prometheus stands on a high rock, and from there calls humanity toward the light.

In the ruined workshop, the observer will notice that all surfaces, despite their chaotic appearance, can actually be used by the actor; for example the slanting rock where Hercules can join Prometheus and free him.

The trunk-like column, a fragment of which can be noticed, is intended to orient the spectator and remind him of the workshop he saw in the first act. This column is that on the left before the workshop is destroyed.

Prometheus, ACT I

Prometheus, ACT III

ECHO AND NARCISSUS

This design was adapted to the dimensions of the hall in the *Institut Jaques-Dalcroze* for the productions given in June, 1920. The spring in which Narcissus admired himself was enlivened by five naiads at its base, spread out in a line, heads turned toward the vertical rock. Each time that the image of Narcissus was reflected in the water, these naiads would murmur in harmony, drawing Narcissus' attention to their looks and gestures. At other times, their silence and their drowsy heads would precisely express the warm silence of the forest during a summer afternoon. A strange thing but a natural one: no one could doubt the presence of water, even though he clearly saw the floor of the hall at the foot of the rock.

In addition to the naiads, the piece included Echo, Narcissus, and five nymphs.

Echo and Narcissus

GLÜCK'S ORPHEUS: THE ELYSIAN FIELDS[1]

Orpheus travels the underworld seeking Eurydice. The scene in the underworld is made up of complicated sets of stairs, broken by terraces; and the whole is held up by pillars fitted into the supporting walls. Accordingly, the characteristic feature of the underworld is *steps*.

If, then, anyone recalls the music that introduces Orpheus to the Spirits, of the Blest, he will understand that only *inclined planes*, without a vertical line of any kind to interrupt them (steps are a combination of horizontal and vertical lines), could in themselves express the perfect serenity of the place. [This refers to the upstage portion of the setting.] Their arrangement is particularly difficult; but, happily, the score gives valuable clues in this respect.

In such a space, physical movement is naturally calm and quiet; and the soft light—with its uniformity and its gentle mobility—transforms the material reality of the actual construction into a kind of rocking movement that is wave-like in its effect. Thanks to the lighting, the characters share in this unreal atmosphere.

[1 Reproduced from the Portfolio, *Adolphe Appia, 1 septembre, 1862—29 fevrier, 1928* (Zurich: Orell-Füssli, 1929).]

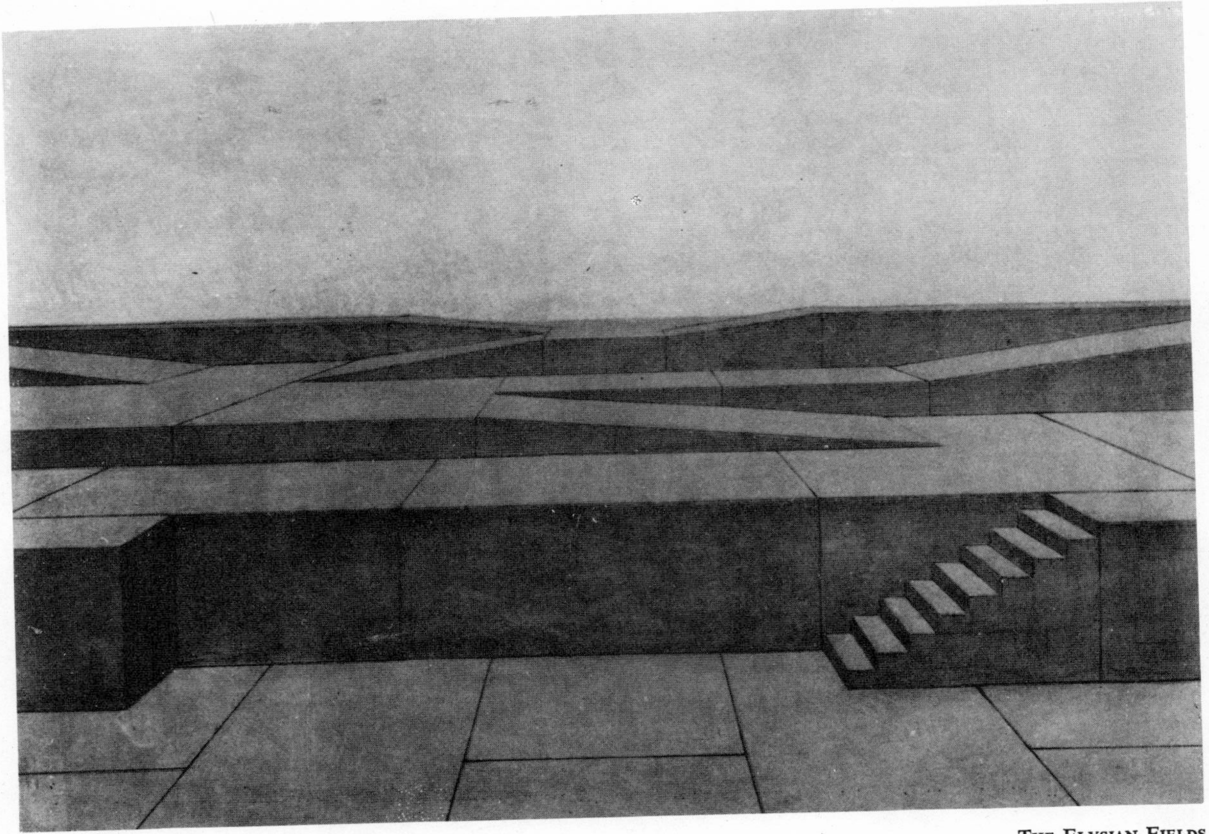

THE ELYSIAN FIELDS

RHYTHMIC SPACES

The following designs, dating from 1909, constitute part of a series of projects initiated by Jaques-Dalcroze, and intended to create a style suitable for establishing the value of the human body under the control of music. Without any other objective, they are a point of departure.

RHYTHMIC SPACE

RHYTHMIC SPACE

RHYTHMIC SPACE

FOREST GLADE

An example of a forest suggested by very simple means—cut draperies and a suitable lighting arrangement. It can be used in any kind of hall, or even in a drawing room. The light is filtered, as necessary or desirable, through hidden cut-outs of cardboard, and the shadows that fall on the characters can thus become mobile. The synthesis is complete.

The three tree trunks in the foreground are probably super-fluous.

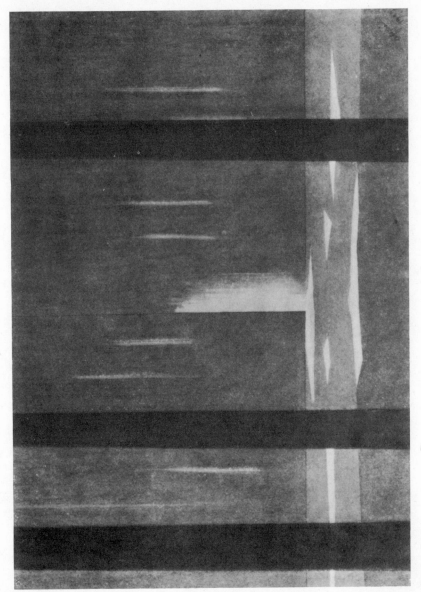

FOREST GLADE

SHADOW OF THE CYPRESS

For this rhythmic space, the author had at first proposed an avenue of cypress trees. Little by little, he removed the trees, keeping only the shadows. Then, finally, this one shadow remained: for this alone is enough to evoke a whole countryside. It is worth noting that the nature of the shadow can be controlled by fluctuations in the light, and that these changes can be made to correspond to a particular musical rhythm.

SHADOW OF THE CYPRESS

MAN IS THE MEASURE OF ALL THINGS

ADOLPHE APPIA'S
"MAN IS THE MEASURE OF ALL THINGS"
(Protagoras)
A Preface to a New Work[1]
translated by Barnard Hewitt

This title is the motto of my latest book: "The Work of
Living Art." It expresses all my thought and distills the principles
which have guided my labor.

An astronomer knows very well that his calculations
concern his eyes and not the stars. When he announces the discovery of a new star, he can only state the day and the hour
when his eyes were able to observe it: the star itself is unaffected
by his mathematical discovery.

The philosopher is aware that his systems only brush the
surface of something which remains forever unknown to him.

The applied scientist makes use of electricity, for example, forever ignorant of what it is that serves him.

The engineer can construct the most colossal machine,
the most complicated mechanism; all his knowledge, whatever
it may be, is gauged by his ambition and by our needs.

So it appears that in every human endeavor, Protagoras'
axiom is the expression applicable to human effort.

However, one main area of our culture, and of by far
its most elevated activity, would like to escape that axiom. That
is the area of Art.

The artist deals above all with an Unknown, whose

[1We do not know what Appia meant by his sub-title. If he contemplated another
book on "living art," he did not write it.]

· 123

presence he finds in nature, or at least in a "nature" which he thinks outside himself.

The painter studies nature in order to reproduce it. Where is that nature?

The architect builds up volumes and arranges them according to his taste. Where does he find his taste?

The poet describes or expresses life and his way of understanding it. Where does he find that life and his vision of it?

All artists imagine that they reproduce and express something presented to their eyes, to their sensibility. They think they are spectators, spectators of themselves, or else of their brothers, or yet of what they call "nature." Their detachment is an illusion. Obviously superior to all other men, because they do not make use of forms established by their intellect for utilitarian ends, or to satisfy their curiosity, they accept the Unknown which forces them to create, without even trying to approach it or to analyze it. For are they not artists!

Now, more than any one else, the artist works under the categorical imperative of Protagoras. For him, more than for any one else, man is uniquely and exclusively the measure.

But what man? Is it man at rest who provides the artist with his measure? Or is it man feeling and thinking presenting himself to the searching eyes of him who wishes to reproduce that spectacle?

Is the artist a spectator, an active spectator to be sure, but nevertheless a spectator?

In art, is life a spectacle? Is art the mirror of life as has been said, and how overwhelmingly?

Is art a work necessarily circumscribed by a process which encloses it and limits it?

We have betrayed ourselves, and at the same time, we have betrayed art—We speak of "works of art" which implies the identity of the art and the work.

We have works of art but do we possess art?

When that question first presented itself to me, like a sphinx barring my path, I was too young to try to answer it, and much too inexperienced to try to solve the problem which it so impassively presented to me.

If art is to be the supreme expression of life, of our life—(we know no other)—it will not be the life of man at rest, not the life of man thinking and feeling. It will be the life of man living, and consequently moving and acting.

Now, all our forms of art, that is all those which produce works of art, are immobile—architecture, sculpture, painting, are immobile by definition.

Life is mobile and active. Our art forms derive from a convention which does violence to life by depriving it of its essential principle.

This would not matter if we had with these immobile arts an art form which expressed life in flux, in action; for then our immobile art forms would become concessions to a kind of perfection which is denied to active life: they would become ornaments to that life.

Do we have this supreme art form? This form which can embrace the whole of life in its passionate rhythm and exalt it into a work of art? And supposing that we have this art form, what characteristic will distinguish it unmistakably from our works of art frozen in their too gorgeous immobility?

I have omitted the musician from my list of artists. It seems obvious that if painting, for example, belongs to the category of fine art, music has no place there! No need to dwell on it.

Music speaks neither to our intellect nor to our eyes. It speaks to our ears; and our hearing functions in time, not in space. In music we have an art for which time, time-duration and its variances, are the condition of existence.

The fine arts exist in Space. Music exists in Time.

"Man is the measure of all things." What is the measure of man in time?

Here we are at the heart of the question.

Movement is our only possible measure of time—Does movement occur only in time? No; movement measures space too.

Thus movement is, through time, the measure of man in space; that is, in Space and Time.

Music measures time only; but our sense of hearing, which perceives music, is an integral part of our total organism. In order to measure space, music must therefore pass through that organism.

The human body, living and moving, will be the medium by means of which we shall rescue the art work from its age-old immobility. And since it is living, the work of the human body—of the incomparable Self—will be no longer an art work but a work of art: The Work of Living Art!

We must still distinguish between any movement and movement become work of art.

Taine tells us—in a formula, somewhat bare, perhaps, but certainly definitive, that "the aim of a work of art is to reveal some essential, salient character, consequently, some important idea, more clearly and more completely than can real objects. It achieves this through a group of parts, whose relationships it systematically modifies."[1]

The spontaneous or voluntary movement must therefore undergo a "modification" in order to enter the portico of art and

[1H. Taine, *Philosophie de L'Art*, 2 vols. (Paris, 1881), I, 41-42.]

126 ·

penetrate its sanctuary—There can be nothing arbitrary in that modification, for art is in essence an obligation.

In passing through our body, music, which springs from an obligation, achieves the transposition of its will into a movement which is regulated by that will. This movement, become peremptory and imperative, will measure space.

Our whole physical organism, if it submits to the laws of music, will thus become a work of art—and thus only.

But there is still another essential difference between the living body and the media of the other arts, the "fine arts."

The living body is no more a brush or a chisel than it is a canvas or a block of marble. It is endowed with consciousness; and that involves responsibility.

If the work of living art carries our total organism into the domain of art—that living organism carries art itself into the domain of the spirit.

That is the obligation which we cannot shirk without failing grossly—how many examples have we had—and falling to the level of the passive, inert instrument.

Music (the musician) is the hand of the sculptor, controlling and directing the chisel. We, *we* are both the chisel and the block of marble—If we do not see in this situation, surely exceptional, a spiritual responsibility, we surrender the rights of a living being; our work of art will doubtless be mobile, but it will not be living.

The movement of a body that has no responsibility—that is the condition of the marionette. It is for us to choose responsibility.

———————

Today all of us feel the inadequacy of the fine arts; all of us wish to give them movement, all of us seek the means.

The idea of "modification," of which Taine speaks, is central to our aspirations toward a living art.

One may propose boldly that the question is summed up in the means chosen to effect that modification, without which there is no work of art.

Rhythm is the sole means of "modification." Rhythm is the hyphen which joins time to space, the temporary life of sound to the fleeting life of movement.

The question grows narrower, becomes still more technical. Thus: what kind of music will address itself most directly, most imperatively to the living body; and what kind of living body will be most apt to understand the language of music and to interpret it submissively in space?

Here we are concerned with education, since we are living and hence responsible.

· The fundamental principle of modern education is not to inculcate alleged knowledge arbitrarily and by force but on the contrary to light in man the fire of understanding so that it may shine forth and permit him to receive in exchange the light from the fires of others. All education worthy of the name must inspire the need for this exchange.

For us, and from the purely technical point of view, the exchange is effected from music to our body—from our body to music, each influencing the other all the way to its primal source.

Music is the miraculous creation of our most intimate and apparently most inexpressible being. The work of living art, which issues from music, can result only from a radiation from inside to outside, which confirms our educational principles.

Therefore we can reject all other methods.

In our time, the Eurhythmics of Jaques-Dalcroze is the only discipline which takes this mysterious and sacred road. Its beauty is a result, never an end. In it we possess the technical means—the exchange, the reciprocal gift. That is its supreme guarantee.

What are its applications?

Our living body can be concerned only with an applied art, that is to say, an art which takes part in life. All art that is expository, ostentatious, or scholarly is unworthy of the living body's high function.

Here we touch on the most sensitive point, and perhaps I may be allowed to conclude this brief explanation of principles by raising some probably unforeseen considerations which will enlarge our view.

———————

I have said that we will be the chisel and the block of marble in the hands of the musician-sculptor. But . . . are we not also the statue? Therefore, the work of living art unites in a single organism the means and the end, the instruments and the accomplished work.

Without the presence of a conscious spectator, a statue, a picture, simply does not exist. Since the work of living art is conscious and responsible, it is self-sufficient.

A human body moving under the authority of music needs no spectator; it is both the work of art and its audience.

Living art abolishes the dualism which has killed in us the great Reality of art, that pitiable opposition in which one man is constantly a producer and the other unalterably a consumer. Living art exists solely by virtue of its own power and without any contribution from a sensibility outside itself.

Living art is not a spectacle.

Nevertheless, living art does not fear to be looked upon, for it lives in broad daylight, thank God! So one may ask what will be the attitude of the spectator faced with a work which is not a spectacle, and consequently is perfectly secure without the help of his presence.

For a long time we have separated art from our life and from our homes, in order to shut it up in museums, concert halls, or theatres. Living art knows not these sad compromises: it lives, we live in it, it lives in us. Living art has restored to us the measure we had lost, the measure of all things: *ourselves!* And if, occasionally, it presents itself to our view, this is only in order to convince us once more . . . And he who looks upon it, looks not upon a spectacle but upon a triumphant demonstration of Life.

No matter in what frame we wish to place living art, it dominates that frame or overshadows it.

If in the theatre, on the stage—our settings, painted and two-dimensional only, suddenly cease to exist. Their measure is not that of a living being: living art blots them out.

Once more "the triumphant demonstration of life" is affirmed! The body, at the behest of music, commands and orders space. Little it cares for age-old conventions, for deep-rooted customs—all must be cut to its measure, all must adopt its pattern. Is not man the measure of all things?

A new technique arises, not arbitrary, but gravely imperious. The body speaks, the body demands; one must defer to it, one must obey.

And the spectator is present at this transformation; he accepts by degrees this high and stern discipline; he consents to the sacrifices it demands of him; within his own organism the aesthetic life awakes. He is no longer a spectator; he becomes a collaborator and understands that he must renounce everything that contradicts the axiom of Protagoras. He wishes he were in the space created by the living body, he too wishes to create that space. Thus he takes part in what he has always regarded solely as a spectacle. He is very close to rising from his seat, leaping upon the stage, participating in this marvelous demonstration of the body's life transfigured by music. Finding himself on the threshold, he ends by wishing to penetrate to the sanctuary: he wishes to *live* art.

I cease for the time. In forthcoming articles[1] I shall describe the various applications of living art, particularly in the theatre and dramatic art, as well as the aesthetic and social reforms which it will draw along in its luminous wake.

---

[1] It is impossible to say with certainty which essays Adolphe Appia had in mind, for he wrote more than thirty after 1923. However, we may disregard those dealing with specific plays and operas, those which he prepared for exhibitions and conferences, and a few others, such as *La Réforme et le Théâtre de Bâle* and *Curriculum Vitae d'Adolphe Appia*. By elimination we arrive at the relatively few in which he discusses problems of aesthetics. Most of these bear no date. Edmund Stadler, in his bibliography of Appia's writings (*Maske und Kothurn*, Graz-Cologne, V. 2, 1959), places these undated pieces in Appia's last years, properly, I believe. They are:
Art Vivant ou Nature Morte, written 1922, published, Milano: Bottega di Poesia, 1923.
Expériences de Théâtre et Recherches Personnelles, written 1922-24.
L'Ancienne Attitude, written 1927 or 1928.
Mécanisation.
Monumentalité.
Pittoresque.
Reflexions sur l'Espace et le Temps.
Two earlier unpublished essays also relate to the aesthetic question with which the two works in this volume are concerned: *Le Geste de l'Art* and *Essai sur un Probleme Dangereux*, both dated 1921.
All of Appia's essays and treatises, a total of about fifty, were given to me by the *Fondation Adolphe Appia*, Geneva, Switzerland, and will be made available in English translation in due time.—*Walther R. Volbach*]